Complete Guide to
Winter
Camping

Second Edition

Complete Guide to
Winter
Camping

Kevin Callan

FIREFLY BOOKS

A Firefly Book

Published by Firefly Books Ltd. 2021
Copyright © 2021 Firefly Books Ltd.
Text copyright © 2021 Kevin Callan

First printing

Library of Congress Control Number: 2021935570

Library and Archives Canada Cataloguing in Publication
Title: Complete guide to winter camping / Kevin Callan.
Names: Callan, Kevin, author.
Description: Second edition. | Includes bibliographical references and index.
Identifiers: Canadiana 2021017207X | ISBN 9780228103523 (softcover)
Subjects: LCSH: Snow camping—Handbooks, manuals, etc. | LCSH: Snow camping—Equipment and supplies.
 | LCGFT: Handbooks and manuals.
Classification: LCC GV198.9 .C34 2021 | DDC 796.54—dc23

Published in the United States by
Firefly Books (U.S.) Inc.
P.O. Box 1338, Ellicott Station
Buffalo, New York 14205

Published in Canada by
Firefly Books Ltd.
50 Staples Avenue, Unit 1
Richmond Hill, Ontario L4B 0A7

Cover and interior design: Firefly Books

Printed in China

 We acknowledge the financial support of the Government of Canada.

Photo Credits
All photos by the author unless otherwise credited.
Paul Kirtley: 2
Tim Foley: 10, 20, 59, 60, 82, 94, 99, 200
Shutterstock: Smit, front cover; nikolpetr, 14; maiciej nicgorski, 16; Chase Clausen, 64; FotoRequest, 186; ClubhouseArts, 188 (black ash); Ina Raschke, 188 (white oak); Jim Cumming, 195, 196 (right); Rabbitti, 197 (right).
Istock: RobThomson, 122; Joel Carillet, 127 (right); konane, 129; txking, 160.
Snowtrekker: 47
Alamy: Nadezda Murmakova, 85; Kevin Walker, 110; Purestock, 113 (top); Janice and Nolan Braud, 113 (bottom); Panther Media GmbH, 115; Clint Farlinger, 171 (left); Dariya Angelova, 171 (right); Nathan Allred, 172; Lorraine Swanson, (174)

Contents

It takes a village to raise a child.

— traditional proverb

Acknowledgments

THE MOMENT YOU CONSIDER YOURSELF an expert in the woods, nature will remind you that you're not! That's why when I set out to write a book on winter camping, I reminded myself that there were a lot more accomplished winter campers out there. The camping community is a close-knit family of amazing and enthusiastic people, and I reached out to them.

I had authors like Hap Wilson, Jon Turk, Jim Baird, Boris Swidersky and legendary winter trekker Garret Conover write up expert advice gathered from epic journeys across the frozen landscape. I asked filmmakers David Hadman, Justine Curgenven and Colin Angus to send me tips and tales from their work on capturing the mysticism of winter. I asked seasoned YouTuber Glen Hooper and weathered outfitters like Paul Kirtley and Paul "Spoons" Nicholls of Frontier Bushcraft, Dave and Kielyn Marrone of Lure of the North to highlight some tips. Musician/winter trekker David Hadfield threw me a tip or two and some lyrics; countless product managers and equipment designers from outdoor companies, including Jim Stevens from Eureka, Margot and Duane Lottig of Snowtrekker Tents, Jeannie Wall of Outdoor Research, and Dan Cooke of Cooke Custom Sewing, were able to help out. Social media friends sent me an endless hodgepodge of their tips gathered from their days and nights spent out in the beautiful, crisp, cold woods.

Put all this together, and you've got one of the best gatherings of sage winter camping advice to date. Enjoy the read, and I hope to see you out on the frozen trail.

Foreword

A FEW GENERATIONS AGO, WHAT has now become known as "hot tenting" was the norm for anyone living or traveling throughout the boreal forest in the shoulder seasons, and winter in particular. Long the province of indigenous peoples; prospectors, foresters, surveyors, trappers, scientists, and adventurers were quick to adopt their techniques to enhance winter travel in the vastness of the northern forests. Calvin Rutstrum wrote about it in his seminal book *Paradise Below Zero*, which was the first time the topic had been presented for recreational winter travelers. To current readers, *Paradise Below Zero* seems short on details because it was written at a time when common knowledge included much of what now would be categorized as bushcraft and rural living skills: skills that need to be taught and practiced, as they have become unfamiliar.

While a few scattered individuals and guides kept the traditions current as active links to a vast body of refined knowledge, it was not until the publication of *A Snow Walker's Companion* in 1995 that a renaissance occurred — one that continues to gain momentum. Due to a gap in the lineage, what was old appears new again, and the rediscovery has inspired several Traditional Winter Camping symposiums in Canada and the US, two of which have celebrated their 20th anniversaries. A number of micro-businesses have sprung up, providing traditionalist gear in the form of tents, clothing, toboggans, tent stoves, and all manner of tools and goods that are not readily available. In North America most of this activity is centered in the Northern Midwest,

Traveling through the wilderness in the winter reveals an absolute dreamscape.

northern New England, and Ontario, in Canada. Most of the other provinces, and a number of boreal countries in Europe, also have regions where interest is flourishing.

Anywhere that would be categorized as canoe country in the open water seasons is snowshoe and toboggan country in the winter. The boreal forests, and the edges of the barrens, provide a vast habitat that is still remarkably wild, with some regions remaining close to true wilderness. While weekend trips and relatively short outings are plenty of fun and eagerly engaged in, some wilderness travelers really live for, and revel in, longer trips that are measured in weeks or months. For the ambitious and lucky few, there are always a few trips underway that span years. A shift in perspective occurs, and what may start out as the development of camping skills takes on a far more expansive view that meshes with living skills, and all the absorbing competencies that make long-term comfort and autonomous self-containment an important part of the experience.

Because the wilderness areas of the boreal forest have not changed much over time, and the seasonal conditions make the same demands whether one is part of a culture that has thousands of years experience living there or is someone seeking the rewards and joys of competent wilderness travel, a highly refined traditionalist approach has much to offer the current recreationist. As our skills are developed, we come to recognize that the current market-driven world of catalog culture is following the trends that evolve out of ever more specialized adventure packaging for generally shorter-term outings, and less by the experience- and technique-driven world preferred by those seeking more autonomous and holistic engagement with the waterways and ice and snowscapes of the boreal wilderness.

Whether you purchase components of an outfit from the micro-businesses that have come into being and filled the void left by catalog culture finding the niche too small to address, or make your gear via a course offered by individual practitioners or a folk-school, or are handy at your own fabrication, there are ways available with which to comfortably engage with an exciting, marvelous winter world. Because the toboggans hold a lot of gear beyond what would be reasonable in a backpack, trips become luxurious within heated tents, with more elaborate meals, complete relaxation with creature comforts, and the option for much longer outings. All of this is vastly different than what cold-bivouac campers can experience. Families with young kids are now enjoying snowshoe and toboggan forays into the Boundary Waters Canoe Area Wilderness of Minnesota, and the Algonquin and Temagami regions of Ontario. I have personally been on a four hundred-mile, 60-day crossing of the Ungava Peninsula in Quebec, where one gentleman in the party was 68 years old at the time. During my guiding career kids as young as 10 have accompanied their moms or dads, and a 78-year-old woman provided the upper age bracket on a trip along the frozen Allagash River in Maine. She took great delight in mentioning a −36°F dawn, as a highlight of that trip to folks who thought she was "crazy" to spend a week snowshoeing and hauling a toboggan in late January.

The winter provides a vast, wonderful world to those who may have seen the region from a canoe and felt the tug of curiosity for the season when Orion strides boldly across the wild night skies. Should the lure of the waterways in the frozen season beguile, let the grand opportunity unfold!

—*Garret Conover*

The snows that are older than history,
The woods where the weird shadows slant;
The stillness, the moonlight, the mystery,
I've bade 'em good-by — but I can't.
— Robert Service, *The Spell of the Yukon*

Introduction

THE CRACK OF THE 12-GAUGE SHOTGUN echoed through the frozen spruce. It was −42° when I fired at the snowshoe hare. I missed, and I was hungry. Neither I nor Charlie, the Cree elder I was traveling with through northern Quebec, had eaten yet that day. So I went to run after the rabbit, hoping to get in another shot. Charlie grabbed my shoulder, stopped me from bolting blindly through a thick stand of alder and calmly suggested we stop for a boil-up — strong tea made over a hot fire.

The problem with Charlie's request was the amount of work involved in making tea in the frozen north. Tea is never made with melted snow. It's made of lake water, gathered by chiseling a hole through the ice. (Tea made from melted snow tastes like burnt milk.) This task takes an hour, if you're lucky. Wood is then gathered, chopped and lit. Energy is spent and hunger gets worse.

We made the tea. I respected Charlie. I didn't understand him at the time, but I did honor him. Even when he called me a "silly over-hyper white man."

The tea was done and I was about to kick snow over the fire to extinguish the hot coals when Charlie motioned for me to reach for the shotgun. "Let's have lunch," he said. There, in front of us, was the snowshoe hare. Northern rabbits keep to their established runs due to the deep snow. That meant the hare would eventually circle back. It did, and I didn't miss this time. The tea and rabbit were divine.

Being out on the land with people who take pleasure in the cold season can be life-changing. The further north one goes, the more common

A black-capped chickadee drops by camp for a snack.

winter travel is. In fact, it's the prime season to go gallivanting in the woods. Most of our southern population cringes the moment it gets cold outside, and when the rare individual heads into the frozen landscape, they're viewed as a deranged explorer tempting fate.

Charlie taught me the opposite. Winter travel is a time to be calm and collected. It's not a time to try and survive; it's a time to live. Allow your body and mind to embrace the cold, not dread it. There is a moment of transition, of course. When you first go from the warmth of your house or car to the frigid wintry air, you second-guess your sanity. Then, gradually, your anatomical furnace kicks in. You adjust, even thrive. Layers of clothes are removed, your body warms and the feeling of being out in what author Calvin Rutstrum labelled a "paradise below zero" becomes highly desirable.

I spent a month traveling with Charlie in the frozen north, helping to check his trap lines and generally being schooled in the joy and freedom of winter travel. Beyond drinking bush tea and hunting snowshoe hare, I made my own snowshoes, anorak and winter moccasins. I roasted a moose nose over the campfire, cooked up a beaver's tail, weaved a bed of spruce boughs and traveled more than 124 miles (200 km) over snow and ice. I was never cold, uncomfortable or miserable, something I can't say for others living in the south. While they were waiting impatiently for winter to be over, I was praying for it not to end.

David Hadfield, singer/songwriter and extreme winter camper, has his own story of how much being outdoors in winter means to him:

"I had a fabulous day once in the winter bush north of Elliot Lake. As I trudged the last mile down the last lake to our camp, I cast around for some way to keep an intimate memory of it. The sound of my snowshoes came to mind, the steady crunch, crunch, crunch as they broke through the thin crust. I kept it in my mind and later wrote the song *Gyproc Box* around it, contrasting the purity and openness of the day we'd experienced with the more typical southern way of living, locked away from all things natural and wild."

Canoeing on a cold day in early spring.

Gyproc Box

The snow falls, and the wind blows
There're no walls, where the land froze
There's black spruce, and jack pine,
Hard rock, and it's all mine
Nothing beats a trail to travel farther
 every day
  I'd rather have lakes and trees
  and rocks
  Than hide away in a southern box
There're fresh tracks, in the white snow.
Where they lead to, only God knows.
There're moose and grouse and
 porcupine,
Otter slides and beaver sign
Lynx and coyote on the go,
Rabbits hiding in the snow

And stretching out behind me is a record
 of my own
  I'd rather have wolf and mink and fox
  Than hide away in a gyproc box.
The axe rings, and the tree falls.
The dead wood, frames tent walls
The stove pops, and the heat spreads.
It warms hands, and it bakes bread
And just beyond the cotton it's 38 below,
  I'd rather have lake and trees and rock,
  Than hide away in a southern box.
And I smile,
When the snow,
Lies deep,
On my land,
Again.
          (from the album *Wilderness Waltz*)

CHAPTER 1

Choosing Partners Or Going It Alone

Choosing a partner

CHOOSING A PARTNER TO GO with you can be a challenge. Problem is, who should you ask? Blindly asking the friend at work to be just as compatible out in the remote wilds could be suicidal, or it could help nourish the relationship back at work. Asking a possible spouse can be a way to perpetually ruin the relationship or strengthen an everlasting bond. Asking a complete stranger is like buying a pair of boots through the mail: they might cripple you on the trail or be the best footwear you've ever owned.

Here's a list of some general rules to follow when choosing and keeping a partner:

- Make sure to prioritize skills and ability before friendship.
- Don't overcrowd the campsite. Keep the numbers down to six or less.
- When a companion drops out at the last minute, you're better to go solo than to randomly choose a fill-in.
- The route and the mode of travel chosen should match the group's general philosophy — don't bring an extreme trekker along on a relaxed trip or a first-time novice on a remote barren land crossing.
- A trip leader must be chosen and agreed upon. They make the final decisions (and are there to blame when things go wrong).

Characteristics you should look for in your teammates:
- Good communicator
- Not selfish
- Does his/her fair share of work
- Dependable
- Sense of humor
- Confident but not arrogant
- Knows his/her limits
- Has good judgment
- Realizes that everyone has his/her own unique character

Going alone

For most, the benefits of traveling solo far exceed the worry of something going wrong. In fact, solo tripping quickly becomes habit-forming and the first danger is that you'll snub all your friends and go out alone all the time. To quote legendary paddler Bill Mason from his film *Waterwalker*, "All of my life, people have been telling me that you should never travel alone… but it's interesting — I've never been told that by anyone who's ever done it."

The benefits of solo travel start with the simple fact that a trip shared with others has to be more deliberate and arranged. Going alone is easier. You can eat what you want and when you want, and travel wherever you want and for long as you like. But it's also a time when your senses are more alive and you find yourself studying the complexities of nature more than ever before. Traveling solo is definitely a life-altering experience. Before you go it alone, however, there are a few key points to consider.

Solo tripping in the winter is a lot more work. Consider that before you go, and where you're going. Hauling gear, pitching the tent, gathering wood, fetching water — it all takes double the time and energy, and you have limited daylight to do it in.

Make sure you are skilled in navigation, wilderness first aid, weather forecasting and survival. Mistakes that occur within a group situation are often manageable. A simple blooper when solo can be deadly.

Most first-time solo trippers attempt a single night. That's one of the biggest mistakes. At first, you're going to be phobic of the unfamiliar and you'll be spooked while sleeping in your tent at night. After day two or three, you'll be so exhausted from not sleeping that you'll start to relax a little. After day five, most of the phobias will go away. By day seven, you are at peace and the real hazard becomes the desire to stay outside and live life as a hermit.

Jon Turk circumnavigated Ellesmere Island on his polar expedition.

STAYING ALIVE

"Imagine the situation: You're in the high arctic. Totally isolated. There is virtually no opportunity for rescue. You've got 750 miles to go. You move forward, or you die. So you're crawling through saturated slush and frigid melt-water pools, soaked to the skin, shivering.

How do you manage this situation mentally and emotionally? The only solution is to shut the mind off. Stop thinking; stop calculating miles to go versus food remaining. Don't even suffer. Just crawl. It's clean. Fundamental. Cathartic. Don't try to preserve your dignity. Dignity is a foreign concept from another cosmos. Crawl."

— *Jon Turk, from his book* Crocodiles and Ice

Solo tripping in the winter can quickly become habit-forming.

Here are a few tips for traveling alone:

Pack lightly. Having no one to help share the load is a problem — that's why packing light should become an obsession. Be prudent about your food intake.

Bring a good book. You'll have a lot of spare time on your hands, especially if the weather turns foul. To keep your mind active and morale lifted, pack something to read. Some favorites for solo travelers are Daniel Quinn's *Ishmael*, Edward Abbey's *Desert Solitaire*, John Muir's *A Thousand Mile Walk to the Gulf* and Kenneth Brown's *The Starship and the Canoe*. My personal pick is Sigurd Olson's *The Lonely Land*.

Tell someone back home your plans for each day. It's even more crucial that you keep to those plans or let someone know of any changes.

Buy, rent or borrow a satellite phone and/or SPOT Personal Locator Beacon. Also, wear a pealess whistle at all times. If you don't bring these emergency devices, then you're playing silly games and giving friends and family back home unnecessary anxiety.

Always consider the worst-case scenario and devise a contingency plan. You might have to pull the plug on your trip at any time. Don't just pack a map of the trip route — add information about the surrounding area as well.

Keep a journal. You'll have moments of deep thought out there. Take advantage of them — jot everything down. Great things have come out of others doing the same: Henry David Thoreau, Noah John Rondeau, Paul Gauguin.

Get a full physical prior to the trip. You don't want any surprises out there. It's not a good time to pass a kidney stone or suffer a heart attack. Besides, your family doctor can help you plan for the trip. My first-aid kit is top-notch thanks to my family physician.

Never listen to people who criticize solo campers for being antisocial misanthropes. Some are, of course. But most are well-rounded, highly intelligent, heart-warming individuals who feel it a privilege to be able to break away from the norm every once in a while.

Taking the kids

Thinking back to when my daughter Kyla was born, I had a lot of friends tell me that my life of traveling in the outdoors was over. They were wrong. It was just beginning.

Before I list the tips that I believe will help make winter camping a positive experience for any kid, I have to share what Kyla has taught me over the years trekking in the woods. She always slowed my pace down dramatically by spending time looking at things like snowflakes and snow fleas. My trips in the past were all about distance. Tripping with Kyla brought me back to reality. I've never been so immersed in the wilderness, so aware of my surroundings than when I'm tripping with her. Who cares how far you go? It's what you experience along the way that's important. She taught me that. Here are a few tips about camping with kids:

Be realistic. The average time young kids can spend hiking is only a couple of hours, at most. They get better as they get older, but don't try to push them. Make every experience a positive one or they won't want to go again. If you don't move up the ladder of progress slowly, your child will definitely come crashing down.

When should you take your kids out camping? The earlier the better.

When to go? The biggest question asked about taking kids camping, especially in the interior, is: "how old should they be before taking them?" My experience has taught me that the earlier they go the better. A child is easier to handle when they are not walking. Many parents decide to wait until they are a teen. That's a huge mistake. No teen wants to spend time with their parents.

Be a parent and a leader. Your child needs direction out there. Explain everything to them, communicate with them, involve them in the trip and never treat them like baggage tagging along on "your" trip. Act more like a guide. Travel as fast as the slowest member.

Be as creative as a camp councilor. Have games, songs and activities prepared in advance and know how to make them fun. Kids don't care about how many bird calls you hear or how nice the weather is. They want to play, be told silly stories before bed, burn marshmallows on a stick, feel comfortable and at home. Make a birthday cake for no apparent reason, hand out small gifts every morning, hand out wacky types of candy for each camp chore they do, bring musical instruments like spoons or a harmonica.

Laugh and don't show fear. Things will definitely go wrong while on a trip — count on that — and your phobias are on high alert when you're with your family. But if you don't laugh at the misfortunes (the moderate ones, at least), or reveal the fears you have of things out there, then they won't either.

You are their role model, and they are little sponges soaking up everything you do and say out there. If you giggle at a tumble or sing a silly song during a bad weather, they will, too.

Remember, we're all different. No one child is the same. All children have different limitations and all parents have various degrees of skills and stress levels. So don't take the expert's advice on what your child can accomplish out there too seriously; this time, you're the expert.

The biggest disadvantage of winter camping with kids is all the extra gear you have to haul.

Taking the dog

An hour after my canine tripping companion of 12 years had been euthanized, I put my feelings about her life on paper. I wrote up a list of Bailey's faults and strengths, her crazier character traits and the stunts she pulled during a life that included more than 600 nights out in the woods. I posted my thoughts on my online blog that evening, and by the end of the next day I had received more than 500 messages of condolences from people who either knew of Bailey or were trippers who also rejoiced in canine company.

More surprising was the number of people who wrote about willingly subjecting themselves to the maddening appeal of tripping in the woods with a dog. Bringing Bailey along was a challenge. I carried her specially designed pack full of kibble and chew toys more than she did. She was the first to have breakfast, lunch and dinner. She insisted the tent be put up for her

JIM BAIRD'S DOG BELLA LOVES PULLING THE SLED

"I've always taken my dogs on winter camping trips with me. Why would you want to leave your best friend at home? Good gear for your dog isn't sold at the pet supply stores. Try www.sleddogcentral.com to source professional sled dog equipment and information. Make sure your dog has an x-back style harness that fits them properly. The less fur your dog has, the warmer a jacket it will need. If you have a male dog, get one with a flap at the rear portion of the jacket's bottom. This is made to protect his penis from the wind on really cold days. (Don't laugh, this is important!). Sled dog booties protect your dog's feet from cuts and scrapes caused by ice. A high-energy kibble made for K9 athletes, or puppies is best. To prevent ice buildup, trim off any excess fur that sticks out from between their pads before you head out."

Make sure to get booties for your dog.

— *Jim Baird, writer and filmmaker*

My dog Angel loves her warm doggy jacket.

immediately once we reached camp. She even rode the winter sled more than she pulled it. Bailey was chased by a porcupine, a lynx, and a hawk. She loved rolling in crap and dead and rotten animal carcasses.

So why did I, and all those other dog owners, put up with having a dog on a wilderness trip? Bailey never left my side. She was a constant companion, no questions asked. My daughter, Kyla, even nicknamed her my shadow. How I miss my shadow. I doubt that tripping will ever be the same without her. Rest in peace, my dear friend.

Dogs are a strange breed. Some are well behaved and considerate, while others are just a plain nuisance, which is why the question of having them join you on a trip is not all that cut-and-dried.

The golden rule is to take responsibility over the dog's actions. Things

like chasing animals or leaving feces behind on a campsite is normal dog behavior. I'm always asked if my dog will leave the campsite through the night. My dog won't because she's trained not to — and she doesn't want to. It's all a routine for her — staying still when I want her to, heeling the moment we spot an animal, heading off the trail to relieve herself, waiting for her dog pack to be strapped on. A dog loves a job and wants to be part of the trip rather than tagging along. It's instinctual.

A trip to the vet is always planned before heading out to make sure the dog's shots are up-to-date and it's in good overall health. Pack a first-aid kit specifically designed for dogs. Place a glow-in-the-dark nylon collar on the dog. Pack the dog its own sleeping mat and sleeping bag or blanket; it will give it a place to go in the tent and keep it warm. Not all dogs are like huskies, bred for cold temperatures. A dog whistle is important to pack. I wear it around my neck all the time and use it to call the dog back to me when she gets distracted — and all dogs will get distracted. Booties for their feet are great to stop ice and slush getting caught in their paws. They'll hate wearing them, but they'll thank you later. A dog jacket is also a great addition — especially if your dog's breed has limited fur and it's not used to the cold.

Route planning

A poorly planned trip in the summer months can cause some anxiety. A poorly planned trip in the dead of winter can be far worse. Here are some key points that will insure an enjoyable — and safe — winter trip.

- Good trip planning greatly increases self-confidence and in turn increases safety.
- Distances in the winter are reduced considerably, so make sure to match them with the skills, abilities and goals of the trip members (don't make it a death march).
- Realize that night comes early, so camp should be set up at least two hours before dark.
- Check the weather forecast in advance, and expect it to change when you're out there.

- Check the terrain you'll be traveling in and get detailed maps.
- Check where to park your vehicle safely (and legally).
- Plan to accommodate group size for campsites.
- Plan on where you will be obtaining water throughout the trip.
- Mark areas where good dry wood can be obtained.
- Know where you can legally camp and where regulations state you cannot.
- Pack an avalanche beacon, probe and shovel in mountain areas.
- Leave your trip plans and dates of departure and return with friends and family back home.
- Pack appropriate gear for the worst-case environment.

When to go — the best time to winter camp

November
Temperatures are usually moderate with possible rain or wet snow. Snow cover is limited for hauling a sled.

December
Days become short and nights long. Snowfall depth ranges and ice conditions are questionable.

January
Snow depth is usually good, nights are even longer and temperatures can be extreme.

February
Temperatures and snow depth remain the same as January up until the end of the month.

March
Days become longer, temperatures are generally milder and snow remains adequate.

April
Snow is dependent on how much fell throughout the winter and travel becomes very spotty.

"I loved the dim, clammy dark of my tent, the cozy familiarity of the way I arranged my few belongings all around me each night."
— Cheryl Strayed, *Wild: From Lost to Found on the Pacific Crest Trail*

CHAPTER 2

Cold Camping Shelters

HEADING OUT FOR A DAY OF SKIING or snowshoeing in the frozen woods is one thing. Sleeping over in it is another. It's what usually stops many outdoorsy types from trying winter camping. They wonder about keeping warm through the long, dark chilly hours and would rather go home to a mug of hot chocolate in front of a roaring fire (or television set).

There's an enormous LIST of shelters to sleep in, from snow caves to heated canvas tents. All have their place. It depends on where you're going, weather conditions, snow conditions, how long you're going for, how much weight you are willing to carry, and how much money you have.

Tents

To "cold camp" means to sleep in a tent without a heat source. This isn't a regular summer tent, however. It should be a four-season model. What makes a four-season structure is a sturdy pole system and tough fabric that can withstand snow loads and heavy winds. Choose a tent with lots of little extras, such as side pockets and a ceiling hammock for gear storage, a center hook to dangle your flashlight or candle lantern from, color-coded clips and poles for easier setup, secondary guy lines for tightening the tent down in harsh conditions, and a light-colored fabric that allows in more light and brightens up your morning after a long cold night.

A three-season tent can work in a pinch if the conditions are favorable.

Four-season tents often have full-length pole sleeves rather than the clips seen on three-season structures. They also have extra guy ropes and parachute cords, providing more staking choices, and heavier, thicker, waterproof material.

Good ventilation is also a key factor. A separate fly over the tent body is important. The more mesh the main structure has, the better. This will reduce vapor from your breath, which

SHELTER TIPS: TENTS

"I often get asked questions about the differences between three- and four-season tents. What are the differences that qualifies a tent to be four-season? Why is there such a weight difference? Must I use a four-season tent for winter camping?

A four-season tent will have common features when built by any reputable tent manufacturer. It has been tested, both in controlled facilities and on expeditions, to meet requirements found at high elevations (alpine) and above tree lines (arctic). These tents must be able to withstand snow loads and extreme winds. This does not preclude them from being used year-round, in fact they make excellent shelters in warmer weather.

All four-season tents will use aircraft aluminum frames and in a design that maximizes strength to handle snow load and high winds. To achieve this needed strength most four-season tents will use four poles or more.

Most four-season tents will use heavier fabric floors with higher polyurethane (PU) coating levels for greater waterproofness. Most often use floor fabrics

The Eureka K-2 XT four-season tent has all the bells and whistles for winter use. Photo: Mark Williamson

will condense over the inner walls. Once the tent warms up, usually in the morning, the ice will melt and rain down on you and your gear. The more ventilation, the more control

over frost. To keep on the safe side, make sure to cover your gear before bed and store a small brush inside so you can sweep the tent walls free of ice crystals. Double doors also vent better than one. Keep the doors perpendicular to the prevailing winds: door zippers are the first place to gain moisture and let the cool wind in.

Tents come in all shapes and sizes, all of which have their merits. First you've got the cabin style. This is extremely roomy, but strictly for campground use only. Then there's the A-frame or "pup tent." It's a classic design that gives you lots of headroom and works well for large groups, but make sure it's well staked down during heavy

will be a 70 Denier (D) nylon, 75D polyester or 150D polyester. The PU coating levels will start around 3000 mm (indicates fabric can withstand water pressure equal to 10 feet/3 m) with some higher.

The walls of a four-season tent will use a breathable fabric with some no-see-um mesh panels that must have solid fabric panels to close them off. Most panels use zippers to close. Breathable fabrics are better at holding in warmth or, conversely, keeping out cold.

All four-season tents will use full coverage fly sheets for weather protection.

Fabrics used on four-season tents will most often use heavier materials as these have been proven over years of use as the most durable. Polyester fabrics of 68D or 75D, usually ripstop, are used with PU coatings no lower than 1500 mm. Four-season tents have larger vestibules with one of the primary uses being a cooking area. This is a contentious issue as it is always recommended that use of any open flame (stoves) be a safe distance from the tents."

— Jim Stevens,
Product Manager, Eureka Canada

winds. There's also the oddball tunnel tent. Its hoop design is characteristic to the old covered wagon, giving you a light, compact tent with maximum floor space. Some winter campers love this style, and others despise it. It depends on the brand. Some cheaper designs, because the style is not free-standing, can feel quite flimsy when a strong wind hits it the wrong way. A top brand, however, will stand up to gale-force winds and work great for heavy snow loads. My choice is the geodesic dome. Its crossing pole structure makes it free-standing (perfect for pitching on top of snow or ice) and quite stable in a wind storm. It also gives you the best space to weight ratio.

Storm-proofing your tent

- Place a ground sheet inside your tent to prevent melting snow from soaking your sleeping bag, making sure it's big enough to ride up the tent walls at least 6 inches (15 cm).
- Waterproof the seams of a new tent with seam seal (Thompson's Water Seal works great).
- Use shock cords rather than the regular nylon cords to peg the tent sides down. This will help relieve stress on the flimsy fabric during heavy wind storms.
- Attach (sew) extra loops to the fly, especially at the front and rear of the tent (attached to tent poles). This will

SHELTER TIP: ANCHORS

"Here is a tip for anchoring a tent on frozen ground with little or no snow. Purchase 6-inch (15 cm) eye screws at the local hardware store. Use an ax or hammer to pound them into the ground as you would a traditional stake. They will freeze solid in the ground. When you break camp, use a spare eye screw and run it through the "eye" and simply unscrew from the ground. No more pounding and pulling and yanking traditional stakes from the frozen ground..."

— *Rhonda Reynolds*

help stop the fly from rubbing against the tent walls, which will definitely cause condensation and leakage.
- Face the door away from the wind. This area, especially the zipper, is the least storm-proofed portion of the tent.
- Tie guy ropes to "dead-man anchors" (sacks filled with snow and then buried a foot deep into the snow).

The Zen of tent packing

There's the "rollers" and then there's the "crammers." The rollers painstakingly lay out the tent, fold it in thirds, place the poles at one end, and then roll everything up in a cigar shape.

The difficulty always remains in getting the darn thing to fit in the storage bag. To eliminate the hassle, use a larger-sized bag and then compact it by wrapping bungee cords around it. Or you could convert to cramming. Simply open up the storage bag and start stuffing everything in. I use two separate compression sacks: one for the main tent and another for the fly. It's not a bad idea separating the two, considering the tent fly is always wetter than the tent body.

Also, most tent damage is done by campers not airing them out the moment they get back from a trip. A tent can be snowed on for days during the trip and not develop any mold. However, the moment it's stored wet for three or four days back home, it can look like a piece of cheese left on the kitchen counter for a month.

Snow structures

Snow cave

Building a snow fort was one of my favorite urban adventures growing up. I'd dig into the biggest snow bank, curl up out of the wind, and pretend I was surviving a wicked storm in the far north. I was darn lucky the snow plow never came by to turn up the snow and bury me alive. Making a snow cave for real while winter camping can be just as dangerous. If it's made right and precautions are taken, however, it can be an extremely cozy place to spend the night.

Choose your digging site that's clear of avalanche danger, drifting snow or even a tree possibly falling on you. The lee side of a small knoll works best. There will be plenty of snow to dig into and away from the prevailing winds. Take note that dry powdery snow doesn't work well. You need deep, settled, stabilized snow. If all you have to work with is powdered snow, then consolidate it yourself by crunching it down with your snowshoes.

To start, dig a 4-foot-wide (1.2 m) tunnel into the hill. Pile the snow downhill. Then dig inward at least 8 feet (2.4 m) and excavate up and out until you can sit up in the cave and have formed a sleeping platform higher than the entrance/exit. The finished product should have a raised sleeping area, a trench leading outside and a wall of snow (or your pack) by the entrance to keep the wind from blowing inside.

Make sure to puncture two or three holes above you to let sufficient air in. You can light a candle (a candle lantern is best) to give you light and some warmth. It's unlikely the candle will

Boy Scouts make home for the night in a snow cave, above left. A quinzee is simply a downgraded igloo that's easier to build, above right.

produce enough carbon monoxide, putting you to deadly sleep. Just don't light a cooking stove inside, and make sure to store your shovel (or other digging tools) inside in case you become the canary in the coal mine.

Snow trench

A snow trench is usually constructed when the snow around you doesn't have the consistency to dig into without collapsing. You'll need at least 3 feet (1 m) of snow to dig into.

To begin, measure your body size, plus a bit more. Keep the size tight. The smaller area you can lie in, the warmer you'll be. Once the trench is dug, remove the snow and pile it up around the digging site. The roof over you can either be a simple tarp placed across and held down by snow along the edges, or you can lay branches across.

Quinzee

A quinzee is warmer than you think, averaging 10 degrees warmer than the outside temperature.

It's easier to construct a quinzee when it's at least –25˚F (–10˚C) — that way you're guaranteed perfect snow to build with. Start off by piling loose snow in a mound 10 feet (3 m) in diameter and 6½ feet (2 m) high, using a plastic shovel or snowshoe. Make sure not to compact it, though. Let the snow settle on its own for an hour or two. This reduces the chance of it collapsing. Then start digging towards the center, keeping the thickness of the quinzee constant by poking a number of pencil-thick sticks, each 12 inches (30 cm) in length, into the walls and roof. The idea is that you'll know when to stop digging when you expose the end of a stick.

Finally, make sure to leave a small hole in the ceiling for ventilation and place a plastic tarp down on the floor. A platform can be built to raise the sleeping area, away from the colder air, and a candle can provide some warmth. The candle also acts as an excellent warning device for a buildup of carbon monoxide. If it begins to sputter or goes out entirely, then clear out your ventilation hole.

Hammock

There's a sense of freedom that comes with sleeping in a hammock, being more exposed to the elements than you would be in a regular dome-tent. I was a bit anxious about hammock camping during the winter. Hammocks can be cold to sleep in if you don't prepare properly.

The first thing to do is to place an inflatable sleeping pad or closed-cell foam

Hammock camping is like your first kiss — it just feels so right. Photo: Kaj Bune

mat underneath you to insulate you from the cold below. Then you place an under-quilt beneath the hammock to provide insulation and serve as a wind barrier. Various manufacturers offer under quilts, and they attach to the hammock by a small shock cord and cord locks. An emergency blanket, which is waterproof and windproof, can act as an effective under quilt if you can't afford a proper one. To keep your feet warm, which aren't covered by the under quilt, pull your down jacket over the bottom end of your sleeping bag. Add to that a good winter sleeping bag and a properly placed tarp over the hammock, and you'll be super cozy.

Rick Dunseith suggests that you use a hammock over-quilt as the top layer of your sleep system. Perspiration moisture condenses and freezes on that instead of on the outer layer of the sleeping bag, and it is easy to take the quilt out and shake the ice off in the morning. It's light, packs small, and provides some additional warmth, too.

Tarp

Paul 'Spoons' Nicholls, Bushcraft Instructor for Frontier Bushcraft, always tries to find a spot for the tarp that has a natural windbreak (i.e., tree line, rock ledge). If you are on a slope, he recommends that you try not to camp at the base or bottom, as cold air will travel down the bottom of the hill and cause a cold well. Try not to camp at the top of a hill, as you will be more exposed to the elements. Take into consideration the wind direction. It is better to have the wind blowing across the front/open of the tarp than blowing onto the back. Wind on the back of a tarp will eddy over it and suck air and smoke into the tarp. Always look up and check the trees for

SHELTER TIP: TARPS

"During winter camping trips my wife and I have used thick reflective tarps, which we used for desert camping. But instead of reflecting the sun, we faced the foil inward. We snugly fit two tarps beneath the fly and over the main body of the tent. The interior tent temperature was several degrees higher and the mesh openings on our 3-season tent were mostly sealed."

— Daniel James Frank

A simple tarp setup can make things a lot cozier. Photo: Paul Kirtley

widowmakers, dead crowns, or anything else that is likely to fall on you.

Have your fire at least one good pace away from your sleeping area/tarp, leaving yourself plenty of room to walk around safely. Choose firewood that is hard and dense for the longest burn. Dry, dead, standing wood is always the best choice, allowing for a hot, smoke-free fire. Collect twice as much firewood as you will think you need and have this in arm's reach of your sleeping area so you don't have to get out of bed to restoke the fire.

Nicholls's preferred sleeping setup during cold weather camping consists of a bivvy bag (British Army Surplus), a full-length sleeping mat (Therm-a-Rest™), a four-season sleeping bag and a silk sleeping bag liner. Placing your rucksack behind your head acts as a good windbreak. It also helps to have a guy line running under the ridge of your tarp to hang up any kit/clothes, to keep them off the damp ground.

Three best tarp knots

I've always found that it's better to know how to tie a few knots extremely well rather than trying to remember a bunch, most of which you'll rarely use. Here are my favorite three that work perfectly for putting up a tarp.

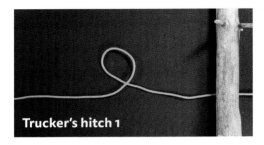

Trucker's hitch 1

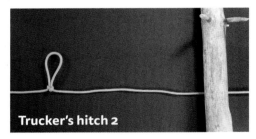

Trucker's hitch 2

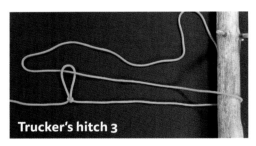

Trucker's hitch 3

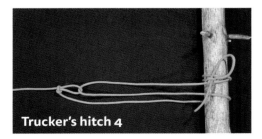

Trucker's hitch 4

Trucker's hitch. This is the ultimate combination of a knot and pulley system. It's a great way to rig tarps and tent guy ropes, or to just tighten up a clothesline in the hot tent. First, tie off the rope onto the tarp or tent corner. Then, about three quarters along, twist the rope to form a loop and bring the loose end of the rope through the loop to form a second loop. Take note that the further away you make the loop from the secondary tie-off source, the more powerful the hitch will be. Now, pass the rope around the other tie-off source (i.e., a tree, a snow tent peg) and bring it back through the loop. Pull and hold down the grip by finishing off with a half-hitch or slip knot.

Slip knot. One of the simplest and most useful knots. It "slips" along the rope and can be easily untied by pulling one end. I use it to secure the rope when attaching it to a tent, tree, or toboggan. Form a loop by twisting the rope and expand the loop with your two fingers. Pull the shorter end of the rope — the tail — through the loop. It should look like a noose. You can pull both the tail and standing line

Slip knot 1

Fisherman's knot 1

Slip knot 2

Fisherman's knot 2

Slip knot 3

Fisherman's knot 3

Slip knot 4

Fisherman's knot. This is the knot known by some as the "improved clinch knot," which is used to secure fishing line to a fish hook (it can also be used for tying down anything else around camp, like a tarp). Run the end of the line around the tree. Then, wrap the free end around the line five or six times. This forms another loop between the first wrap and the space between the tree. Feed the free end through that loop and pull to tighten. The experts say it's the only knot that won't let the fish get off — unless it breaks the line, of course.

simultaneously to tighten your slip knot. To untie the knot, you just pull on the tail, which unravels the loop. The slip knot is generally used to tie around something, like a tree. For this method, you form the loop by wrapping the rope around the tree and then sliding the tail through, between the rope and the tree.

"I love the scent of winter. I love the scent of winter enough to suffer the cold for it."
— Tiffany Reisz, *The Scent of Winter*

CHAPTER 3

Hot Tenting

H OT TENTING beats COLD camping, hands down! I remember the trip that changed everything for me. I was camping in Ontario's Algonquin Park, sleeping in my four-season tent at the end of a long and cold February day of snowshoeing through deep snow. I had no heat source except for my own body heat. It was –17°F (–27°C) when I crawled out of my frozen tomb in the morning. Getting up and getting moving on the trail was the only thing that was going to thaw me out, but the bindings of my snowshoes (and my boots) had a thick layer of ice to chisel off first before I could get anywhere. With frozen fingers and toes, I made slow progress to my vehicle parked at the access point.

The next year I splurged and bought a "hot tent" and wood stove — a canvas-walled dwelling that turns into a sweet oasis when the stove is roaring. It can be –22°F (–30°C) outside and a balmy 68°F (20°C) inside. Moments during an early morning when you're sitting by the wood stove, sipping on hot coffee and munching on baked biscuits, and especially able to pull on de-iced boots that have been hung and dried overnight, are absolute bliss.

I never did abandon cold camping completely. I've packed my four-season tent, even a bivvy bag and all other forms of sleeping in the cold, for mid-March trips when temperatures aren't so frigid. Cold camping does have its advantages. You're not burdened by too much gear and can travel a lot further during the day. Setup and breakdown of camp is also far less time-consuming. In an hour you can be fed and bedded down for the night. With hot tenting, you have to set up the bulky tent and stove and spend a good hour finding and cutting enough wood for the night.

Hot tenting is preferred for times when you just want to be out for longer (and more comfortable) times in the winter woods. It doesn't matter where you are, as long as you're not home waiting for the colder months to end. Distance traveled isn't part of the equation, but length of time is. You can stay out for a serious stretch when you have a heat source to escape to. To me, that's what winter camping is all about. To relish in the silence of winter, getting away from the crowds and enjoying a time of year that few wilderness enthusiasts get a chance to experience.

Material

Canvas breathes. That's the beauty of it. A great amount of vapor is formed inside the tent from your breathing and your gear hanging to dry. The cotton material allows the moisture to escape. This is especially true when you light up the wood stove inside. The heat literally pushes the moisture out through the canvas walls.

Duane Lottig, owner of Snowtrekker Tents, tells his own story about hot tenting:

"20 years ago I started designing tents because I couldn't find a winter

RECTANGULAR WALL TENT
"As someone who almost lost interest in camping a few years ago and now owns my own canvas tent to go winter camping in, I think that getting out there is really important. I feel pretty accomplished! I can make instant hot chocolate and sit in a tank top when it's −4°F (−20°C) outside."
—*Hailey Sonntag*

The more the merrier. Canvas-wall tents, like 18-year-old Hailey's first hot tent, can be built in all shapes and sizes — with some fitting six to eight campers at once.

Nylon fabric is windproof, waterproof and a lot lighter than canvas. Photo: Dan Cooke

NYLON HOT TENT

"My hot tent is made with 1.1 silicon-coated nylon. It is 10 feet (3m) tall, with a 5½-foot-tall (2m) vertical door for easy entry. The fabric is windproof and water-proof. Condensation will occur on the outside wall, but by keeping the top of the door partially open with its double zipper, condensation has not been a major issue. I have made an insulated floor for it and it allows the folks to be in stocking feet at −30°.

Its height gives room for drying items in the top and allows for standing up fully, even for my 6'6" friends. At 6 pounds (2.7 kg) total weight with poles, and with the tent being able to pack down to a volleyball-sized stuff sack, it is a joy to pack."

— *Dan Cooke, Cooke Custom Sewing*

After one night sleeping in a hot tent rather than a cold, confined tent, you'll never look back. Photo: Duane Lottig

hot tent that I was happy with. Hot tent camping was a way to take our young sons winter camping and be assured that they had a positive experience. Hot tent camping is not so much camping in the winter as it is living outdoors in the winter. It reduces our need for warmth to a basic level and frees us from the complexities and stresses of the 21st century, even if it is only for a short time. The warmth and comfort of a heated cotton canvas tent in winter is a joy to experience and share. The friendship and camaraderie that comes from sitting around a warm wood-burning stove on a cold winter night creates memories that will last a lifetime. Spend one night in a heated tent when it is −22°F (−30°C) and winter will soon become your favorite camping season."

HOT TENT FLYSHEET

"It snows at the least convenient times — not when you want it to! — and that's the reason to use a flysheet. A flysheet helps keep snow off the tent in winter.

When it snows, and you're inside with the stove going full blast — glowing and comfortable! — and you are not using a fly, there's no real problem. The heated roof of the tent melts the snow and it mostly runs off. But if you are packing up, or going to sleep, or if it's after breakfast and you are planning to go for a day-hike, a snowfall is a problem. Sooner or later, as the tent cools down the snow stops melting. At that point, it freezes onto the fabric of the roof. As it sticks there, the snow that's still falling also sticks. None of it runs off. Weight accumulates.

If you're not there to beat it off, or fire up the stove again, the fabric will rip or the tent-poles will break.

A traditional wall-tent setup uses a ridgepole cut from the bush, preferably a standing dry straight jack-pine. The tent is suspended from this, tied tightly at 16-inch (41 cm) intervals or so. The flysheet is thrown over the top, and thus separated by 6 inches (15 cm) or so from the tent itself. This distance is maintained as you tie-out the sides. If done correctly, there will be no place where the tent and the fly are

A flysheet over the canvas tent is a real bonus in wet and mild weather, especially with an accumulating snow load.
Photo: David Hadfield

touching. This results in the fly being cool, staying below freezing, and snow never melting or sticking. The flysheet size should be 2 feet (0.5 m) longer than the tent up on the ridgepole, and a lot wider than the tent's footprint.

Another very handy aspect of the flysheet is that it allows a quick-and-dirty winter camp. You can simply tie a line very tightly between two trees (use a trucker's cinch with a carabineer), about 5 feet (1.5 m) up, and haul it as tight as you can to reduce the catenary sag of the line. Throw the flysheet over. Let the sides of the fly touch the snow, tie them out to bushes and whatnot, and then walk around it and heap snow on the edges to get a wind-proof seal. This does not produce a heated space, but with one end closed off and a source of heat at the other [end] it can be surprisingly comfortable."

— *David Hadfield*

Hot tent designs

The canvas hot tent has been around for a long time, and there's plenty of different designs used by various cultures around the world. However, winter campers make general use out of three basic designs: the rectangular wall tent, the walled pyramid tent, and the modified wedge/A-frame.

The bonus of pyramid tents is that only one center pole is needed. That means a quick setup and set-down, and one incredibly light tent to haul. Photo: Tim Foley

Rectangular wall tent

My first hot tent was this design (see page 42). I lived in it for a month while working in the north. It was spacious and had lots of headroom. I had weekly baths by using a blow-up kids' pool and water heated on the wood stove. I didn't travel anywhere with the tent, though. It stayed at my basecamp the entire time. Setting it up was too labor-intensive; I had to cut timber for at least seven poles — one center pole, two scissor poles on each end to hold up the ridge pole, and two side poles. It also had so many guy ropes used to keep its form that the lashings looked like some massive spider web. Due to its open, rectangular shape, heavy winds would shake the tent something fierce as well. But it was a cozy home — even at –40°.

Pyramid walled tent

Pyramid tents come with one huge advantage. They're set up with just one center pole. The pole can be cut on-site or an aluminum pole can be packed along. The sides are held out with guy lines. The bonus to this means a quick setup and set down, and one incredibly light hot tent. I've tripped with an Atuk tent and an Esker Arctic Fox 9' x 9' (2.7 x 2.7 m), both that weighed only a mere 13 pounds (6 kg). They're also amazing at holding up against high winds, which is why they're the top choice for polar explorers.

Some models of pyramid tents come with the wood stove set in the middle, and the stove pipe going straight up through the top. Other designs have the wood stove to the side, by the front door, and the pipe exiting to the side. If you choose the model with the stove pipe going straight up then make sure it's high enough that sparks don't land on the tent, creating burn holes. A spark arrestor helps with this. However, running the stove pipe up the center has never been an issue. Maybe I'm just super paranoid. Of course, having the stove in a central spot does provide a comfortable sitting area for a group of campers wanting to all gather around the stove for an evening chat and nightcap.

Modified wedge/A-frame tent

This is a self-supporting style tent. Lightweight shock-corded aluminum poles are packed along to form the frame and the canvas is pulled over it. It has fewer guy lines than the other two designs. It also has less headroom than the rectangular tent, but not by much.

This is my tent of choice. I own three, made by Snowtrekker: Expedition Shortwall 3 Person — 9' x 11.5' (2.7 x 3.5 m), Expedition Basecamp 2 Person — 8' x 10' (2.5 x 3 m), and a 7' x 8' (2 x 2.5 m) Minimalist (yep, that's a lot of tents). Snowtrekker makes one of the lightest and best

designs out there. For group trips I use the 3-Person Expedition Shortwall. It weighs 22 pounds (10 kg) and gives you a lot of space. For lighter two-person trips for me and the dog, I pack the 2-Person Expedition Basecamp, which I find gives you more headspace, and when just on my own I pack the Minimalist, weighing just under 10 pounds (4.5 kg).

Snowtrekker's Expedition Shortwall is my tent of choice.

Tent floor

Pitching camp is the same as cold camping. You pack down an area with your snowshoes. Of course, it's a much larger area than a four-season tent. Hot tents don't come with a floor, so you'll have to create one. The traditional style is to line the tent floor

with conifer boughs. I prefer balsam. It's a weed tree, easy to find, cut and gather, and you end up smelling like a Christmas tree by the end of your trip. Don't use white spruce — you'll end up smelling like cat pee by the end of the trip. I weave the boughs together like a

Balsam boughs make a perfect tent floor — as long as you're in a remote area and not a managed park.

picnic basket made by a kindergarten art class. They give you a soft cushion to sleep on, create a warm airspace below you, and allow loose snow from your boots or a spilled cup of tea to sift through, keeping the floor clean and dry. Take note, however, that some government parks frown upon winter campers cutting boughs. In that case, you'll have to pack a tarp. Try to find a non-slip type. The regular Polytarps you get at the hardware store are the worst choice. They're slippery and you'll be head-over-heel in no time.

For a floor, Rick Dunseith recommends some of those 2-x-2 foot (0.6 x 0.6 m) rubber mat puzzle pieces from the hardware store, the kind you can put down in a kids' playroom. Cut them in half and cut off the scalloped edges, and bring about four of these 1-x-2 foot (30 x 60 cm) pieces with you. They are great for kneeling on in the snow, setting up your kitchen and they make useful seat cushions. They are very light and inexpensive.

HOW TO MAKE A TIPI, CHRISTINA STYLE

"I decided I would make my own tipi-style hot tent so I could camp in the cold, but still stay cozy.

I wanted the tipi to be 10 feet (3 m) in diameter and 10 feet (3 m) tall. I bought nine poles, 10 feet (3 m) long and ¾" (2 cm) in diameter. They were strong but not too heavy. I brought the poles home and put them together as a traditional tipi. I added a wooden ring, so it resembled an umbrella: the poles would go through the holes, be affixed with a cotter pin, so they could be removed and transported, and then the smoke could escape through the hole in the center.

The best deal for canvas was to use painter's drop cloth. I purchased two 12'-x-15' (3.6 x 4.6 m) pieces that were sewn together, to make a piece 12'-x-30' (3.6 x 9.1 m). The pattern was drawn on and the canvas was cut. I put grommets at the top to hold the canvas onto the wooden ring. The grommets would slide onto a bolt that was sticking up from the ring, so the canvas could be easily put on and removed. I sealed the two ends with Velcro and strings, and made the door with a steel ruler and some magnets, so it could open and close easily. The tipi has since been renovated with the poles being halved, making them

transportable by sled for backcountry camping. The bottom was replaced with green plastic-coated canvas to avoid snow sticking to it."

— *Christina Scheuermann (a.k.a. Camper Christina), winter camper blogger*

Buying a hot tent can be costly. Making your own can be far less expensive, and it gives you lots of bragging rights when the temperature drops and everyone heads back to their cold, unheated nylon tents. Photo: Shawn James

Wood stoves

There's just as many shapes and sizes of wood stoves as there are hot tents. What you're looking for is one that has a main box, legs that fold out, and sections of pipe that fit inside for storage and travel. If you have a rectangle walled tent or a modified wedge/A-frame, then you'll need a pipe elbow to lead the other sections outside the tent. The first section of pipe also needs a damper.

The main body of the stove is made of stainless steel, averaging 24 gauge. Some are made of titanium, making an extremely lightweight but insanely expensive stove. The pipe sections are galvanized steel, 26 gauge.

The fold-out legs raise the stove from the snow base. To limit the heated stove melting into the snow and becoming dangerously unstable, I place a heat reflector under the stove. A fireproof mat or layer of firewood can also be used as a base. I also place two chunks of wood (called skid logs) parallel under the legs to create a more

A wood stove is a welcome treat on cold nights.

A wooden base placed at the bottom of the wood stove, above left, and a tripod to hold up the smoke stack, above right, add greatly to your safety.

solid base. The stove is placed a good 20 inches (0.5 m) away from the tent wall. I place my firewood around the sides to prevent wind blowing the canvas towards the stove, but not close enough for the wood pile to catch fire.

The pipe hole in the canvas tent is lined with a sheet of fibreglass material to stop the canvas igniting. When using the rectangular or modified wedge/A-frame tent, you'll have to hold the stove pipe up with a tripod made of two 6-to-8-foot (2-2.5 m) lengths of wood, held together with twine to keep it upright.

The stove is used for a heat source and as a cooking surface. I prefer a side plate that attaches to the stove. It provides a place for cooking pots, pans and kettles. I'll even hitch a reflector oven to the side for baking bread and pastries.

The size of the stove you use inside the tent varies with the size of the tent. The larger the tent, the more volume to heat, the larger the stove. My smallest stove (Muskrat Metalworks) fits my two-person tent and is only 9 inches (23 cm) long, which allows it to fit sideways on my toboggan. Of course, the size can be a disadvantage. You end up having to cut the wood into smaller pieces. Also, if temperatures are going to be –22°F (–30°C) to –40,° you'd have to burn a lot of wood. But for normal (cold) temperatures of 14° to –4°F (–10° to –20°C), the stove works out fine. The total weight is 6.6 lbs (3 kg), with a height of 15 in. (38 cm). The chimney consists of five sections of 3-inch (7.5 cm) diameter

Colin Angus cycle toured in extreme Arctic conditions. It may not be as appealing as spring in Spain, but with proper preparations it can be quite enjoyable.

EXTREME CONDITIONS

"I once cycled thousands of kilometers through Siberia during the winter. Temperatures of –50 degrees Celsius were common. At –50, all sorts of strange things happen to everyday items. Mercury thermometers are useless, because mercury turns solid at –38. Propane can't be used, since it's a liquid and not a gas at such temperatures and therefore won't flow. Likewise, we discovered our Jetboil stove was impotent — no jet and no boil."

— Colin Angus

pipe that stacks together for convenient storage. However, one of the biggest benefits this stove has is that the front draft doubles as a fire-observation window. It's the closest you're going to get to a glass front window on a camp wood stove — and it's my favorite feature of the stove.

Stove maintenance

First things first. You have to burn off the poisonous gases in the zinc formed when lighting up a new stove. Don't breathe this stuff in. It's nasty. Once the fumes are gone, she's good to go. Not much can go wrong with the stove while you're using it. It's when you store it that the problems begin. Rust will set in. I really tried to keep my first stove from rusting — problem was, I stored it in the backyard shed. Moisture grabbed hold and I had one rusting stove in less than a year.

You can scrub it with steel wool and apply blackening compound, or paint it with black heat-tempered wood stove paint to reduce the rusting. You can also wipe it down and smear vegetable oil on it after each use. Eventually, it will still rust. The main thing is to control it. Don't leave soot and ash in the stove. It may contain moisture and start a chemistry experiment while the stove is in storage.

When you buy a stove, you might see a note from the manufacture stating you must layer the base of the stove with sand to eliminate/reduce the bottom rusting out. I did that on my first trip: I packed a bag of heat sand with me. It was a naïve and silly move. A false bottom made of metal (a lot lighter than a bag of sand) can be purchased to help strengthen and protect the metal on the stove's base. The open space below the flames also aids in creating a better fire and a lot more heat.

What about spark arrestors? Some hot tent winter campers swear by them and some swear at them. A spark arrestor is designed to reduce the amount of hot sparks flying out of the stove pipe and landing on the tent's canvas. However, they tend to clog up quickly, collecting creosote, especially if you're burning lots of resin-heavy wood like pine and spruce. Either clean them on a regular basis or just make sure your stove pipe is long enough and/or angled away from your tent.

All-night burn or midnight freeze?

Here's the dilemma: do we keep the fire in the stove going all night or let it burn out? There are two schools of thought regarding fire maintenance inside a winter canvas tent. One is to keep marginal warmth throughout the night by having a "volunteer" crawl out of his cozy sleeping bag and stoke the stove with more wood. The other is to have the unfortunate volunteer rise first in freezing temperatures and spark the fire again.

I've always followed the second school, and having a weak bladder, I'm usually the one to unzip my frost-covered bag and dance a jig around the tent as I fumble for kindling and matches. My regular winter camping partner, Andy Baxter, has a far weaker bladder, however. He "volunteers" to keep the fire going until morning. His reward is the right to the first cup of coffee (spiked with the Baileys Irish Cream).

Hot tent safety

The idea of being confined inside a canvas tent heated by a roaring wood stove appears quite hazardous. I guess it can be. Things can go wrong. The two main concerns are carbon monoxide poisoning and having the tent burn down. Both are quite rare — but both can happen.

Carbon monoxide poisoning is the less likely of the two. Hot tents are well vented. My Snowtrekker canvas tent has two vent holes at either end, and I always zip open the front door a bit before going to bed. The stove itself is the main way that toxins are removed from inside the tent. It sucks fumes outside. Once the flames go down at night, the stove will start leaking carbon monoxide. As long as the tent isn't airtight, fumes will still escape through the stovepipe. Just ensure the stovepipe is exiting the tent away from the prevailing wind. You don't want smoke blowing down the pipe and into the tent.

You definitely don't want your tent burning down. It's your heat source and escape from the freezing temperatures. Even if you're able to escape the fire, you'll still have to survive the cold night.

Fires can happen when candle flames touch the tent wall or when the wood stove is not properly managed. You can use LED flashlights to light up the tent or contain the candles in a candle lantern — that's a relatively easy fix. With the stove, the first priority is to make sure the pipe sections are properly secured. You don't want them to separate while the stove is at full burn. (Some hot tenters prefer to wire their pipe sections together for this reason.) Also, make sure to set the tent up out of the wind. You don't want the tent walls and stovepipe moving around uncontrollably. Always have leather work-gloves ready to handle the stove, or if a pipe becomes separated.

Usually, the main issue when it comes to a woodstove is human error. It's very close quarters inside the tent, and it's very easy to stumble onto the stove. Not only could you be badly burned, but you could also hit the stove and separate the pipe sections. That would be disastrous. Communicate with your tentmates. Tell them when you're going to move about. Place your hand on someone's shoulder to help keep balanced.

Another issue is knocking against the stove while you sleep. I burned a gigantic hole in my sleeping bag on one trip. I'm a restless sleeper, and sometime during the night I rolled over and touched the bottom of my sleeping bag on the stove. Thankfully, I wasn't burned and I used duct tape

Bivy bags make exceptional lightweight shelters for winter backpackers. Photo: Shawn James

to patch the hole. I now form a barrier of wood upright in the snow, creating a fence around the stove. I also make sure not to store my woodpile too close to the stove. It can ignite if the stove gets too hot.

So, what's the safety procedure in case your tent burns down? Escaping quickly is the first priority. When I go to bed, I always keep my flashlight handy — and a knife, so I can cut myself free if I have to. Like in a house fire, always keep low to the ground. Most important, however, is to store safety gear outside the tent. Never

have all your gear inside the tent. I have the following items cached near my toboggan, just in case:

- SOL escape bivvy bag
- SOL emergency shelter
- First-aid kit
- SPOT emergency communication device
- Matches and fire-starter
- Warm jacket
- Wool layers
- Extra footwear
- Warm gloves

CHAPTER 4

Clothing and Supplies

Clothing

KEEPING IN MIND THAT your body heat is what's actually keeping you from freezing, the type of clothing you wear is crucial. But before you go out and spend your life savings on high-tech fashion wear, remember that old-timers survived months on end in the cold without the aid of Gore-Tex or Polypropylene.

The trick is TO dress in layers. Start off during the cold morning temperatures looking like a walking puffball if you like, but as you generate heat through exercise, peel off the layers to avoid your sweat freezing to your skin.

It helps to know how your body loses heat when trying to understand why you're cold. There are six basic principles.

Conduction. You lose heat by having direct contact with something that is cold. To grasp that concept, grab a metal fuel bottle with your bare hands and you'll feel a burn from the fridge temperatures.

Convection. Think wind chill. It might not be too cold, but the wind cuts through you like a knife. Add to that by wearing cloth next to your skin that is saturated in your own sweat. Yikes!

Radiation. The warmer the object (i.e., your body during physical activity), the more heat that radiates away from you. If you have proper clothing to block radiation, the better you are.

Three different materials to help keep you warm. From left to right: cotton anorak (author, Kevin Callan), Merino wool (Tim Foley), polar fleece (Ashley McBride).

Evaporation. You lose heat the more you perspire.

Respiration. Every time you take a breath, you lose heat that your body created; then you breathe in cold air. Cover your mouth with a balaclava.

Urination. If you have to pee, then pee. The longer you hold it in, the more your body has to keep the urine warm.

Steps to stay warm
Next to the skin. This is the base layer, and the most important element to fight the chilled-clammy feeling.

What it comes down to is wearing something that doesn't make you sweat. Cotton is bad, very bad. Choose a two-piece long underwear set made from fabrics such as polypropylene, silk or even that non-itchy Merino wool.

Insulating layer. This is the layer you're taking on and off all day and night to keep warm or to cool down. Wool is perfect; Merino wool is amazing; fleece works great and is lightweight; and a down jacket or vest will never fail you (just don't get it wet). Down won't keep you warm if wet.

A cotton anorak is one of the most useful outer layers to protect you from the bitter cold wind. It's totally breathable, not trapping your sweat underneath.

Main shell. This should not be your main insulator; save that job for the insulating layer. It also shouldn't be a big puffy jacket. The outerwear must be "breathable" and must protect you from the cold wind, which is why Gore-Tex type material works so well. It should also come with an assortment of zippers to allow for ventilation.

Renowned adventurer Justine Curvegne suggests that the main issue in winter camping is keeping warm. It's inevitable that the base layers you are wearing will get sweaty and damp, so always keep a dry set of clothes to wear at camp. No matter how wet and stinky my 'thermals' are, I make myself put them back on the next morning to preserve my dry clothes for the next camp.

Jeannie Wall, product developer for Outdoor Research, likes hardshells for durable waterproof protection. They are soft, stretchy, and breathable. The laminates used are more active in their moisture transfer and, by allowing some airflow to come through in microscopic amounts, they offer a much, much more comfortable environment inside your hardshell while still keeping you dry from the outside.

Traditional cotton anorak

Another main shell option is the traditional cotton anorak. It's true that cotton is the worst thing to wear as an inside layer. The material soaks up moisture. But as an outside layer it breathes better and vents moisture away more than any other common waterproof breathable fabric. Moisture is absorbed from your body, pulling your sweat through your inner layers. Basically, it pushes out moist air and excess heat. It obviously gets wet from your sweat, but you can dry it fairly quickly around the fire at night. Even if it doesn't dry out, the anorak is not an insulating layer; it's an outer protective layer. It acts as an excellent

windbreaker while trekking across a windswept frozen lake. Mine is trimmed with coyote fur — ethically harvested from an old fur coat from the secondhand store. I also added a voyageur waist sash to keep things tight and provide a place to hang my over mitts. The traditional design has no zippers and is just pulled over your head, fitting loosely over your other layers.

Rain gear

It seems odd to pack a rain jacket (and pants) on a winter trip, but don't count on it being cold and dry all the time. I've had it rain on me plenty of times throughout the winter. It's the most dangerous time for hypothermia to set in. Just make sure to have a rain jacket that vents properly.

Pants

Wearing blue jeans is just a bad idea. You'll freeze. You need something that will dry fast but not too light of a fabric that the cold wind will cut right through, and they have to be loosely fitting so you can wear long underwear underneath (or not). If you can afford wool pants, you're set for life.

Boots

Choosing what to wear on your feet isn't as easy as one would think. There are just too many types of snow conditions to just strap on one big pair of winter boots and hope your feet stay dry and warm.

Pac boots

Pac boots are the overall common choice. They're the big clunky ones with a rubber bottom, a leather or nylon upper and a felt liner. There are lots of models to choose from. Just make darn sure the felt liner is removable. You'll want to bring an extra liner to slip in when the other one gets wet. Drying your liners in a hot tent is a nightly routine. It's not so easy to dry them out while cold camping, however. Sleeping with them in your sleeping bag will do the trick. The other advantage of removable liners is that you'll be able to wash the nasty stink out of them when you get home. I also place an extra insole in the bottom of the boot. This makes the world of difference keeping your feet warm.

Insulated hiking boots

Another winter boot design to consider is an insulated winter hiking boot. They're great for a mixed bag of winter weather and long-distance hiking. Generally, they end above the ankle, not as high as a pac boot. They don't provide as much insulation as a pac boot and don't come with removable liners. But the boots are breathable, waterproof, comfortable and extremely lightweight for such

From left to right: down booties, overboots, insulated hiking boots, pac boots.

a warm winter boot. They also have a better tread system, and they're perfect for fitting into a high-tech snowshoe binding. Wearing a pair of knee-high gators would be a great plus to deal with deep snow or slush. The biggest bonus for me is the extra insulation in the toes. My toes are always the first things to go numb in cold temperatures.

Rubber boots

Slipping on knee-high rubber boots with a removable felt liner is a good option when you know you'll be dealing with wet snow or slush. They're not as warm as a pac boot or as breathable, but they'll keep you drier. There are no laces to deal with and some models have a nylon covering with a pull strap to stop snow going down your boot. I also find they fit in snowshoe bindings better than most pac boots. Just make sure they fit loose enough to keep your toes warm, but not loose enough to rub and give you blisters.

Mukluks

Mukluks, or what some winter campers call "winter moccasins," are the warmest, lightest and most comfortable footwear I've ever worn for winter camping. They consist of a leather bottom and canvas upper. It's an amazing feeling, walking on snow with no thick barrier between you and the frozen

In cold, dry conditions, mukluks are the most comfortable footwear possible.

ground. They also fit perfectly in a snowshoe binding, unlike a clunky pac boot. Your feet and toes move freely, keeping them toasty warm, and there's less moisture built up than inside a pack boot. I place a felt liner and insole inside, with a good layering of merino wool socks.

Mukluks do have a major disadvantage, however. They are not waterproof. If conditions call for wet snow or slush, then I'd either leave them at home or wear some type of waterproof overboot. They can be slippery in some moist snow conditions as well. I'd suggest getting a pair with some type of rubber non-slip bottom. But if the snow is cold and dry, then mukluks are the best footwear for winter trekking.

KEEPING YOUR FEET WARM AND DRY

- Wear vapor barrier socks. They contain all the moisture, allowing your insulated socks and boot liners to stay dry. The vapor barrier sock is thin and easier to dry.
- Instead of expensive vapor barrier socks, you can keep your socks dry by wearing plastic sandwich or oven roasting bags under your socks. A shower cap works as well. The bags will hold most of the sweat closer to your skin and keep your feet warmer.
- Thicker doesn't mean better. A layer of thinner, well-fitting socks is less likely to cut off circulation and keep your feet a lot warmer than one big sock.
- Avoid cotton socks. They quickly get wet with sweat and create cold feet.
- Wear wool socks, especially Merino wool. They keep you warm and keep the smell down. Wool fibers are hydrophobic and hygroscopic, repelling and absorbing water at the same time.
- Pack a few toe warmers. They're lightweight and can make a real difference on a cold day.
- Place insoles in your boot liners. It makes a world of difference.
- Pack lots of extra socks. One pair per day isn't excessive.
- Start warm. It's more difficult to get your feet warm when placed in cold boots. Store your socks and liners in your sleeping bag to ensure they're warm for the morning.
- Keep your core warm. Once your vital areas get cold, your body will slow blood flow to the more "disposable" parts.
- Dress your feet up in layers: lightweight wicking sock, lightweight wool sock, medium to heavy wool sock.
- Make sure your boots are sized properly. Not too loose, but definitely not too tight.
- If you're going to be standing in one place for a long period of time, then place an insulated pad under your feet.
- Once you feel your toes turning numb, do some jumping jacks or run down the trail for a bit. You'll be amazed how a brief period of physical activity increases warm blood flow to your extremities.
- Don't take the boot companies' temperature rating to heart. I'd add at least 10 degrees to what they're stating.

Overboots

I spotted my mail carrier wearing an overboot called Neos Adventurer a couple of years back, and I've been packing them on winter trips ever since. The boot works as an overshoe. I'll pull them on over my mukluks or leather hikers when the snow is soft and wet — perfect for snowshoeing, ice fishing or winter camping. The sole gives amazing traction, and even though the overshoe makes you look like Herman Munster, they're extremely lightweight.

Down booties

Down booties are perfect for wearing inside the tent. The moment I set up camp in the winter (or sit by the fire with a single-malt at home), I put them on. What a cozy feeling, knowing you don't have to put on your big snow boots just to step outside the tent for a bathroom break. The bottom grip is decent, down insulation gives them their incredible warmth and the extra height ensures snow doesn't find its way in while you're walking back from the outhouse.

Hands and head

Warm hands, warm heart

My pinky finger is cursed. Years ago while working in forestry, timber cruising in northern Ontario, I got severe frostnip on my left hand's baby finger. Now, the moment it gets damp or cold, it burns and throbs. The older I get, the worse it gets. I seriously think that's the only thing that bothers me while winter camping. I've never really been hypothermic, never got cold feet. But my darn pinky finger drives me crazy.

I roll with the punches, however. Protecting my hands from the cold has become a number one priority. First, I wear mitts instead of gloves. Mitts keep your appendages all together, easy to move around, and help them keep each other warm. Gloves keep them separate and cold. I like leather better than synthetic — only because synthetic will melt while you're dealing with the camp stove or fire. Leather is also pliable in the cold. On the trial I'll wear a forearm gauntlet-style with liners. If I heat up, I'll just wear the liners and hang the main mitts like a schoolboy, with a piece of string tied to each and laced through my jacket and around my neck. Leather mitts get wet more than synthetic. Make a habit out of drying them every night by the fire.

I do wear leather gloves for camp chores (cooking, tending the fire,

CAMERAS

"The biggest challenge is keeping the cold from zapping your camera batteries. Batteries are fine with the cold, you just have to warm them up before using them. I keep my batteries close to my body while I'm not using them and ensure that they are warm before I turn the camera on. On really cold days, this means taking the battery out of the camera between shots and putting it in my warm mitts. Despite all these precautions, batteries will drain faster in the winter so consider bringing extras.

Cameras don't like humidity. Moving from a cold and dry outdoor environment to a warm indoor environment can create a lot of condensation as the camera warms. The most drastic option to deal with this is to put the camera in a sealed Ziploc bag before you bring it inside and to leave it there until it has warmed up. Next is to just bring it inside but not use it until it has warmed up and been dried off. And another option is to simply leave the camera outside in a proper protective case overnight. Just remember to warm those batteries before you use them."

— *David Hartman (Haywire Films,*
Keepers of the Wild)

A wool toque and ski googles help keep the chill out while you're crossing exposed windy lakes.

cutting wood). My fingers aren't cold while I'm working and my blood flows out to my appendages. I just use a pair of winter leather work gloves with a clothed back and wrist covering; you can purchase them at the hardware store. They're perfect for gripping a hot kettle or cutting up brush for kindling.

Head gear

Keeping your head warm is important. For mild days, I just wear my wool toque. On colder days, I wear my Elmer Fudd "mad trapper" style hat with ear flaps. On extreme days, I add a Merino wool balaclava. Add a pair of ski googles to protect your eyes, and you're set for walking across the windswept frozen lake at −40˚.

WINTER CAMPING CHECKLIST

- ☐ Tent
- ☐ Ground cloth
- ☐ Snow stakes
- ☐ Sleeping bag
- ☐ Air mat/pad
- ☐ Snow shovel
- ☐ Ax
- ☐ Saw
- ☐ Candle lantern
- ☐ Headlight (extra batteries — lithium)
- ☐ Change of (long) underwear
- ☐ Wool hat
- ☐ Wool or fleece
- ☐ Insulating jacket
- ☐ Rain jacket and pants
- ☐ Fleece pants
- ☐ Insulated boots
- ☐ Gloves
- ☐ 3 pairs of wool socks
- ☐ Balaclava
- ☐ Camp stove/fuel
- ☐ Cookwear
- ☐ Eating utensils
- ☐ Plastic trash bag
- ☐ Waterproof matches/butane lighter/fire rod
- ☐ Fire starter

- ☐ Meals and snacks
- ☐ Dish soap
- ☐ Pee bottle
- ☐ Water bottles
- ☐ Map and compass
- ☐ GPS
- ☐ 30-50 ft. parachute cord
- ☐ First-aid kit
- ☐ Lip balm
- ☐ Sunscreen
- ☐ Personal medication
- ☐ Extra glasses or contact lens solution
- ☐ Fishing/hunting license
- ☐ Personal ID
- ☐ Repair kit
- ☐ Survival kit
- ☐ Personal locator beacon (SPOT)
- ☐ Avalanche beacon and probe (if traveling in possible avalanche area)
- ☐ Camera
- ☐ Assortment of Ziploc bags
- ☐ Hand/feet warmers
- ☐ Snowshoes

- ☐ Skis
- ☐ Knife
- ☐ Sunglasses/ski goggles
- ☐ Whistle
- ☐ Water purification kit
- ☐ Toothbrush
- ☐ Biodegradable soap
- ☐ Toilet paper

Other items:
- ☐ _____
- ☐ _____
- ☐ _____
- ☐ _____
- ☐ _____
- ☐ _____
- ☐ _____
- ☐ _____
- ☐ _____
- ☐ _____
- ☐ _____

Survival kit

Survival kits are important to bring along, especially when heading away from base camp. They have to be minimal, but provide you with means to start a fire, boil water, make shelter, navigate, signal for help, perform basic first aid, catch a fish or trap an animal, and fix gear.

To keep size and weight to a minimum, which allows you to keep the kit on you at all times, follow the survivalist code of the "rule of threes." In three hours you can die of exposure; in three days you can die of thirst; in three weeks you can die of hunger.

Here are my essential survival items, which I store in a waterproof metal container (the container itself can be used as a cup or cooking pot). Some items can be eliminated to cut down weight and bulk, depending on how you're traveling. Just keep the "rule of threes" in mind when doing so.

- Heat-reflective blanket. I upgrade to a small survival bivvy during the shoulder season. SOL (Survive Outdoors Longer®) offers a wide range of survival blankets and bivvys.
- Paracord. I purchased a product called Fish 'n Fire Cord. It's seven-strand 550 paracord with eight-pound-test fishing line and jute-twine blended inside the

cordage. The fishing line can be used for catching fish and the twine can be used as a fire starter.
- Rain poncho or industrial-sized garbage bag. You'll need more than just a bunch of branches and leaves to keep your shelter dry.
- Fire-starting kit, including a lighter or waterproof matches and/or fire steel and fire starters.
- A knife. Of course, you should already have a knife (and fire steel) attached to your belt or hanging around your neck.
- A compass — and knowledge of how to use it.

A sharp knife is a safe knife.
Photo: Paul Kirtley

I wouldn't go camping, especially in the winter, without some kind of locating device such as the SPOT.

- Water purification tablets. These tablets, like Aquatabs, are effective and smaller to pack than a water filter.

- Fishing line — even dental floss works. And a few fishing jigs.
- Aluminum foil, used to craft a makeshift fishing lure and then to bake the fish in the remaining foil.
- Emergency locator beacon, such as those from SPOT or InReach. Make sure to pack extra batteries.
- Whistle. Remember, three strong blasts is a distress signal.
- Mini-flashlight and batteries.
- A small pencil (for leaving notes) with snare wire and duct tape wrapped around it.
- Small first-aid kit — and take a first-aid course every few years. It's better to be equipped with knowledge than a bunch of gear you don't know how to use.

Repair kit

"No problems, just solutions." That's a good statement to keep in mind when things go wrong. Of course, it's also a good thing to pack a repair kit as well. It doesn't have to consist of too many things, especially bulky things. Just make sure you pack one. You can count on something breaking while you're out there.

- Patch kit (Seam Grip seam sealant glue and collection of patches) for repairing the air mat, tent, boots...
- Sewing kit for cloths and canvas tent (a sturdy needle and a spool of waxed dental floss works great)
- Assortment of screws, bolts and nuts
- Needle-nose pliers or multitool
- Pipe clamp (for fixing poles)
- Snare wire (for fixing stoves, sleds and anything else that needs to be lashed together)
- Different sizes of cable ties
- Duct tape — lots of duct tape

"Snow flurries began to fall and they swirled around people's legs like house cats. It was magical, this snow globe world."
— Sarah Addison Allen, *The Sugar Queen*

CHAPTER 5

Pitching Camp

CHOOSING A WINTER CAMPSITE involves different logic than picking a site in the summer months. In fact, most parks stipulate that winter sites must be at least 30 meters away from existing campsites for two good reasons. First, most summer sites are exposed to the wind. Second, there is rarely enough wood available nearby to fuel a continuous fire.

I prefer lowland swamp areas. They're less exposed to the wind, flat, and have lots of dead and dry standing wood to cut. They're also places you'll never have a chance to pitch a tent in the summer, and they happen to be better places to spot wildlife.

Rule number one is don't pitch camp in an avalanche area or where dead snags or trees can topple down on you. Choose a flat open area.

Staking the tent down in the snow is a lot more challenging. Snow isn't as solid as bare earth. Use snow stakes (or ski poles, snowshoes, sticks, pieces of gear), looping the guy lines around the stakes and burying the stakes in the

snow. Compact them down with your boot, and eventually the stakes will freeze into position. To finish them off, pile snow around the tent to help hold them down. When camping on snow, sturdy snow stakes work much better than puny pegs. If you don't have snow stakes try filling plastic bags with snow, tie them to the guy lines and bury them. These become incredibly strong as the snow freezes.

If you're using a four-season tent, then dig a pit under the front vestibule. This gives you a place to sit and take your boots off before crawling inside and a place to store extra gear under the tent fly.

Top: Tramping the snow down with snowshoes helps settle the snow and makes setting up camp so much easier. It's the very first thing to do after a day of traveling. Above: Adam Ruzzo made himself comfortable out there and spent a month in this homemade shelter, weathering winter storms, bitter cold and a few critters trying to move in with him. He said he'd do it all again in a heartbeat.

Lighting up the night

It gets dark early during the winter months. That's why you'll want various ways to light up the night. Candles are perfect for inside a tent. They even help heat the interior. Just be careful they don't touch the walls, especially the canvas of a hot tent. More tent fires are started with candles than a wood stove. If you're cold camping, candles still illuminate the outside kitchen area while you're preparing your evening meal. Beeswax is the best; they last a lot longer than regular wax candles. It's also best you purchase a candle lantern to keep the flame contained. They can be purchased at most outdoor stores. I pack one that holds three candles at once. It's a bit bulky in the pack, but gives off as much light as one of those old Coleman gas lanterns.

You'll also require a head lamp. Not a flashlight — you need to keep your hands free for camp chores or kept in your mitts for warmth. Also, use lithium batteries. They work best in cold temperatures. Double AA batteries will either drain quicker or simply not work.

Sleeping systems

Just like dressing for the day, your equipment and the process of layering is what will keep you warm at night.

First thing to consider is the type of insulation for your sleeping bag: down or synthetic. The debate over the two is a complex one. Down (the soft plumage of a goose or duck) is lighter, warmer and can be compressed far more than any synthetic bag. Synthetic is usually cheaper, retains its loft better, can be cleaned easier, and if it gets wet it will still give off warmth. If a down bag gets wet, its insulation ability will be reduced more than 80 percent. If you do choose down (my personal choice) than take note of the bag's "loft power." A 400-450 fill is usually made of duck down and is a low-quality bag. A 650 to 800 fill is goose down and is exceptional quality. Anything in between is usually a mix of duck and goose down and matches its moderate price range. Go for the mummy shape and stay clear of the rectangular. You want less air space in the bag to keep warm. A hood is mandatory, and so is the "scarf" located around the neck area and a draft tube along the zipper. Watch the temperature rating given to the bag. Just because

Sleeping pads and a good sleeping bag are essential ingredients to a good night's sleep.

it states it's a –30 degree Celsius bag doesn't mean you'll be warm in such a temperature. Everyone has a different comfort sleeping zone.

Sleeping pads are essential when sleeping on the snow. I had mine deflate on a winter trip, and even though it was only a balmy 23°F (–5°C) outside and I had a –22°F (–30°C) sleeping bag, I got a major chill from the cold ground. There are lots of choices: open-cell foam, closed-cell foam, combinations of both, inflatable mattresses. Get the pad that will

keep you higher off the snow and one that you can afford. I also add under my pad a 6-foot (2 m) length of reflective pipe insulation purchased at the hardware store. It's cheap and effective.

Kelly Gray has a good idea: when setting up camp, sit the tent in a deep snowbank. Walk around with the showshoes to compact the snow and create a firm pad to set the tent up on. Even only a few inches of compacted snow under the tent makes for a much warmer night than a tent set up on bare ground. Leanne Hennessy recommends that you put hot pocket hand warmers in fleece glove liners and place them inside your sleeping bag. They act as mini heating pads and will make your bag toasty. Michelle Brunette has another trick: if you are having a campfire, take a rock from the outer layer of the fire pit (one that is pretty warm, but not scalding hot), wrap it in a sock and put it at the bottom of your sleeping bag when you settle in for the night. Toasty toes on the coldest nights.

Bedtime rituals

You will rarely have difficulty staying warm during the day on the trail, but the night air brings a bone-numbing chill. Here are a few ways to keep yourself more comfortable.

Daylight is greatly shortened during the winter months and it usually takes much longer to set up camp, so be prepared to end the day early.

Choose to camp in a well-protected forested area, well away from the wind and blowing snow. Even better is a swamp. It's out of the wind and provides plenty of dead, standing wood.

Make sure to provide a lot of ventilation inside the tent. Condensation will quickly form from your breathing and cause the interior of the tent to become completely covered in a layer of fine ice particles, which will eventually melt and soak everything inside.

For extra insulation, pile up snow around the sides of the tent with your snowshoes or small plastic shovel.

The moment you finish setting up camp, change into an extra-dry pair of long underwear and dry socks (keep a spare set in the front pouch of your parka so they are nice and warm to put on) and wear a wool tongue to bed.

Smooth out the snow under your sleeping area as soon as possible. Once the snow starts to melt and then freeze it becomes too difficult to flatten. Also, create a shallow trough for your body to reduce rolling back and forth through the night.

Sleep on a thick foam pad or Therm-a-Rest™ (not an air-mattress). Your body will definitely lose more heat to the cold ground than the air.

Fluff your sleeping bag (a top-of-the line, high-quality winter design) before crawling in. The action creates more air space between the fibers or feathers.

Your breath moistens your sleeping bag. Keep your head outside of it and wear a toque to bed.

Use a homemade fleece liner to increase the efficiency of your sleeping bag — or just double up two sleeping bags.

Use a reflector bivvy bag on the outside of your bag to increase the warmth.

Munch on high-calorie snacks just before bedtime. The fuel your body has to burn off will help you stay warmer.

Go to bed warm. Do a few jumping jacks before going in the tent or ride an imaginary bicycle inside your bag.

If you find yourself shivering inside your sleeping bag, put on your rain gear to act as a vapor barrier and hold in your body heat.

Stuff your boot liners in your sleeping bag with you at night to make them toasty warm for the morning.

Store your electronics, batteries or even camp fuel in your sleeping bag to protect them from the cold.

Try to keep your head out of your sleeping bag. Moisture from your breath will get trapped and dampen your bag. Instead, wear a hat with a balaclava or wrap a scarf around your face.

Keep an empty (well-labeled) water bottle inside the tent to pee in. A full bladder robs the body of more heat than an empty one; and besides, who wants to crawl out into the cold night air to relieve themselves at two in the morning?

Women can use a device called a Pee-Mate or Wiz-Easy to help out the aiming process.

Sleep with a hot water bottle, or at least a thermos or Nalgene bottle of hot water for extra warmth and so you have something warm to drink in the morning.

Stuff the next day's clothes inside your sleeping bag.

A candle lantern will light up your tent and give off some heat as well.

SNOW CONDITIONS

"Snow in the bush is not wind packed, and it's often shaded, and will be deep, fluffy, soft, and you tend to sink. Also in the bush, snow will get perched up on air pockets created by shrubs and logs, and the effective depth of the snow due to this airy base can be double the actual snow depth. You may find yourself walking up a micro slope, which is really a pile of logs, only to fall through into an air pocket almost to your chest, even though the snow is only 2 to 3 feet (1 m) deep. In these conditions you will want very large and wide snowshoes for maximum floatation.

On windswept lakes, the snow consistency gets denser and effectively shallower. But it can also get a wind pack crust on top covering a soft airy interior, making trudging very hard work as you have to lift up and over the wind crust with every step, instead of swishing your snowshoes along easily in dense 'sugar' snow.

Lakes, roads and open trails which receive a lot of sunlight will develop a denser consistency snow than shady areas. When the crusts start forming in mid to late winter from freeze-thaw events, the shady areas will have less crust and you will sink lower, whereas in the sunny areas you might be able to cruise along the top of the crust like a snowshoe hare, or the lynx that is following it!"

— *Glen Hooper, extreme winter trekker*

Winter backcountry hygiene

Pooping in the winter isn't as bad as you think. It's also a lot more hygienic and environmental than summer pooping. Simply dig a small "cathole" in the snow, well back from camp. Then you squat over it and hope everything happens relatively quickly. When you've done your business, make sure to ignite the toilet paper and let it burn until nothing remains. This guarantees a fast and environmentally friendly breakdown of the waste material come spring. You could replace T.P. with a snowball. It's effective and even more environmental. I've tried it and haven't been a big fan, however. Other winter campers I know think it's the best method, acting like a toilet bidet. You decide. Just make sure that before leaving, mark the spot with a stick upright in the snow to let others know you've been there; a scattering of poop spots are better than one large communal one.

Pooping in the winter isn't as bad as you'd think. Just hope it happens quickly.

Make sure to appoint a designated pee spot. There's nothing worse than a scattering of yellow snow around camp. Once you're done, kick some snow over it to keep things tidy.

The trick to safe food handling is to make it hassle-free to wash up (or to guilt everyone into making sure they wash up). The best overall method for hassle-free washing is to have two cleaning kits: one stored with the kitchen gear and the other in the toiletry bag.

The kit in the kitchen gear is a no-brainer. The cook will see the hand soap and/or alcohol hand sanitizer among the pots and pans and most likely make use of it before preparing a meal. If they don't, other campers will surely notice and most likely make a comment.

The toiletry bag is the problem. Individual campers can say they've washed up, or even pretend to do so, but who is to say they actually did (yes, this happens more than you'd want to know)? So the trick is to hang a communal toiletry bag in a tree, or somewhere just as obvious, the moment you set up camp. It should consist of the usual items, such as toilet paper, wet wipes,

Dishwashing is always given to the person who didn't make the meal, or possibly the person who made a really bad meal.

and a flashlight. Then attach a second bag with alcohol hand sanitizer. The entire kit should also have a big red bandana or bright yellow ribbon tied to it. Give instructions to the group that when someone has to use the facilities (whether it's an outhouse at the campground or a designated area in the interior), the toiletry bag(s) goes with them. This works twofold: it will allow some privacy to anyone who's using the facilities — basically, if the toiletry kit is gone, then no one else is allowed to wander off to accidentally witness someone pooping in the woods. This also gives a bit of indirect peer pressure from members of the group to make sure everyone uses the hand sanitizer.

The most effective way to wash dishes is to fill a large cooking pot or lightweight collapsible basin with warm, soapy water (use biodegradable soap). For a scrub brush, use a handful of pine needles. It sounds crazy, but pine needles do a better job than wet sponges or scrub pads, which are breeding grounds for bacteria.

Once the dishes are done, take the grey water well away from the campsite and dispose of it in a small hole in the snow. It will become part of the soil come spring. Food scraps or leftovers can be burned in a hot campfire or packed out in a separate sealable plastic bag or container.

One last process to make sure no one gets sick from bacteria on the trip is to place the dishes on top of a small ground tarp and pour boiled water over them. Then, let the dishes air-dry rather than use the same drying towel repeatedly, which is also a breeding ground for bacteria.

Washing up is important. I'm not sure why so many winter campers neglect their personal hygiene the moment they're out there. It's commonplace to see people stop brushing their teeth, cleaning behind the ears, or even washing their hands after a bowel movement. The results of not keeping clean can be a real bother. For example, 25 to 40 percent of all illnesses can be traced back to not washing your hands properly before eating (or having someone touch the communal dish towel after relieving themselves). The obvious way to eliminate this hazard is to use hot water and soap when washing up. The problem is hot water is a rarity when you're winter camping. Generous amounts of hand sanitizer are a good replacement. Make note, however, that it contains alcohol and will evaporate quickly. If it's really cold out, you'll freeze your hands. I also make good use of antibacterial moist towelettes for cleaning up your private parts.

Cleanliness is next to godliness…but this is just crazy. Photo: Dave Marrone

Campfires

What is it about campfires? Why are they so vivid in our memories of camping out? The flickering light, sparks spiraling into the night sky, the warmth radiating from the inner circle. To say the appeal of a campfire is that it gives us warmth and light would be correct, but not the complete reason. It may be that it connects all of us to our primitive times when our ancestors depended upon the heat it generated for pure survival.

Campfires do give us a great sense of community. Whether there are two or ten people circling it, the ones involved in this simple act are able to connect and discuss issues of the world more easily than at a coffee shop or sitting on a bar stool back home. Group dynamics isn't the sole reason, though. Solo travelers enjoy a campfire just as much as a group — even more so, actually. It gives them a sense of security, nightly entertainment and a feeling of calm.

I think it's the feeling of calm that's the biggest benefit. Campfires give us a lot of pleasures, but the very idea of sitting around a campfire, whether it's in a group or alone, is what signifies that you've finally begun to slow down. Your senses open up. A campfire starts to sound good, look good and smell good. You can distinctively hear the snap of exploding resin, watch as the flames change color as it absorbs oxygen, and smell the wood smoke being emitted from logs of maple, birch or pine.

Put simply, the lighting of a campfire signifies that your time spent in the wilderness has begun, and putting it out signifies it's all over.

Finding firewood

Gathering wood for the fire, especially in the winter, is an art form. You need to identify the species and know which is better to start the fire and which burns hotter and longer. My favorite fuel for an evening fire where I live, the near-northern part of Ontario, Canada, is dead and dried maple, oak or ironwood. It's a piece that's too old to be considered a sapling but too young to be mature. If you're lucky you'll come across ones still standing, the ones that can easily be pushed down, dragged back to camp, and sawed up into arm-size pieces. When cut up and burned these species of wood have an extended flame time, great for cooking or just keeping the chill out during a ghost story or two. They also stack well and make an inviting site for anyone using the camp after you. Make sure the inner wood is dry, however. Place your lips to the wood to feel for moisture. Trust me, it works.

Camping in swamps provides plenty of dead, standing wood to keep you warm at night.

Down to basics: an ax and a saw to gather wood, and birchbark to help get the fire going.

Conifers, like pine or spruce, are best to get your fire lit. They don't burn long, but they ignite quick and clean. A bundle of dry, dead twigs taken from the base of the evergreen works perfectly. Conifers contain pitch or resin, which helps them combust. Add a few strands of white birch bark and you'll get the fire started. Dry pine needles, a glob of pitch squeezed from balsam blisters or a piece of dried lichen are also good natural fire starters; or use a homemade fire starter and place it at the base of the fire ring. I like to gather tinder when I find it and not wait until I get to the camp site. Birch bark is a no-brainer, but what many overlook is spruce pitch. The black, hardened, brittle chunks don't get wet, light easily and burn for a long time.

You'll need a base first, or the fire will just burn down through the snow. Cut a few arm-sized green logs and place them down horizontally. Then light the fire on top of the layer of logs.

The trick with fire lighting is to start small. Place pencil-size twigs in a crisscross pattern over the fire starter material. This is called the log cabin design. Some campers prefer the teepee design where the wood is stacked upright. Both work, but I'm a true believer in the log cabin approach, which allows more oxygen to feed the flames.

Place the larger pieces on top, but make sure there's plenty of space for the fire to breathe (too much smoke means you're smothering the flames). Next, place a few more pencil-sized twigs on top to lock everything in place. Ignite the fire starter material with a match stored in a waterproof container (to make sure the match is dry, place a cotton ball on top of the matches in the container and briskly run the match through your

Good, dry tinder can be gathered from the base of an evergreen tree. Photo: Adam Ruzzo

Homemade fire starters

- A cotton ball dipped in Vaseline and stored in a waterproof container
- A strip of inner tube
- A ball of steel wool
- Strips of wax paper
- Pieces of wax crayon
- Birthday candles or what's called "tea lights"
- Sawdust or dryer lint dipped in paraffin and stored in an egg carton
- Strips of duct tape coated with a few squirts of bug repellent (this is my favorite)
- Squirt of alcohol-based hand sanitizer

hair before igniting it to draw out any moisture). A match is better than a butane lighter in the cold.

Lastly, construct a second pile of wood around and even on top of the fire to constantly dry out your fuel source.

FATWOOD

Finding this in the woods is finding gold. It's the resin soaked heartwood of coniferous trees. It's best found in the stump of a dead, fallen tree. When the tree dies, the resin settles down at the base. The outer wood will rot and go soft. But the center wood will contain the hardened sap of the tree. That's your golden nugget. You can also locate fatwood at the base of branches on dead coniferous trees, which can be easier to harvest. Saw the branch off right where it's attached to the tree. That's where the resin would have settled when the tree (or limb) died. You'll see the dark colour of the wood, and it will smell of turpentine. Now split it and make shavings from the wood. It will ignite quickly, even when wet.

Best way to light a fire in the winter

There are many ways to build a fire. Some are common techniques used by backwoods travellers and campground users. The teepee method is common. Lean sticks up together in a cone shape and ignite from the center. Then there's the traditional log cabin, where you stack four walls of wood and ignite from the center. Campers have debated which is best for years. But some campfire techniques are better than others for winter camping. You are lighting a fire on a base of snow, or ice, which melts. That's something to think about. You also want it to light fast, to get warm fast. You also want it to burn as long as possible and give off the most heat as possible. So, here are the preferred winter camping fire designs.

Upside down fire

This one has been called various things (top-down fire, council fire, platform fire) but the premise is the same. You place a layer of large diameter wood on the snow base, then layer it by crisscrossing smaller and smaller bits of wood, making sure the layering process is precise and spaced out (but not too much) to allow oxygen to get to the flames. Make a tinder pile on top, light it and allow the fire to burn down, rather than up. It will last for a long time and give off a substantial bit of heat.

Parallel/hunter fire

This is a simple build but one of the best to cook on. Place two large logs of the same size parallel to each other, slightly apart. The fire is lit between the logs, and your cooking pot is rested on top of them. It's a slow burn, but the flames can be adjusted by adding more tinder between the large logs.

Star fire

This is a good choice if you need a fire burning through the night to keep you warm. Place five or six big, long logs pointing out from one another, like the spokes of a bicycle wheel. Place tinder at the center and push each of the logs towards the center as they burn.

Lean-to

This is perfect for when there are high winds and snow. Place a couple of large logs to act as a windbreak, then lean smaller kindling on it perpendicularly. Now build a smaller tipi fire under the lean-to. It's also a good idea to place a center stick and raise it up now and then, like a leaver, to allow more oxygen flow.

Swedish fire torch

Some call this the "Canadian Candle," but I think the Swedish invented it. You use just one large diameter log. Split it into four elongated pieces/ wedges. Place them back together again, with a half-fist gap, and stand them back up right. You can hold the pieces together with small diameter twine. Then you place kindling in the gap and ignite it. Continue adding more kindling as the main logs begin to burn. This design produces a slow burn, perfect to cook on. Just place your pot or frying pan on top. Keep an eye on it though. It's tough to keep the fire oxygenated.

The Swedish fire torch produces a slow burn, perfect to cook on.

POCKET BELLOW

A couple of deep breaths blasted down into the coals through the EOG V3 Pocket Bellow will get any campfire going. This thing works! It's a blowing device that looks like a hollowed out car antenna. I've never seen such a simple piece of camp gear that really follows through with its promise.

Of course, there are a lot more options to feed oxygen to a flame. Fans made from pot lids or Frisbees, funnels made from birch bark, or even lung-power puffed out straight from the mouth and into the smoldering flames. None, however, are as effective as the Pocket Bellow.

The collapsible rod is made of stainless steel. It also has interior stops to prevent the entire rod from pushing or pulling beyond its limit. That's a brilliant addition.

"A crude meal, no doubt, but the best of all sauces is hunger."
— Edward Abbey, *Desert Solitaire*

CHAPTER 6

Food

TRUDGING THROUGH DEEP SNOW ALL DAY, or just trying to keep warm in your sleeping bag at night, requires a lot of energy. You'll need at least 2 pounds (1 kg) of food per day, per person. Eating a low-fat diet is not a good idea. Indulge in fat.

There's little to worry about when it comes to food spoiling, but anything that contains water needs to be avoided. It will freeze. Lettuce becomes wilted, eggs become slushy. Meals like bacon, stews, chili, shepherd's pie, and the like are good options for winter cold-weather camping. Pre-cooking the main meals is also a very good idea. It can reduce water content (and weight) and saves a lot of time in camp. Remember, the sun goes down quick during the winter months.

If you're cold camping, the fewer steps and less time you take to prepare your food, the better — not only because it's too darn cold to be bothering with extensive cooking times, but because the fuel for camp stoves burns off a lot quicker in colder temperatures. If you're hot tenting, however, cooking meals becomes the highlight of the day. The possibilities are endless when using the wood stove for cooking.

Sandwiches for the day (PB & J, honey, lunch meat, cheese, chocolate-hazelnut spread) can be made up in the morning and kept in an insulated bag with a thermos of hot water for coffee, tea, soup or hot chocolate. Flat bread, English muffins or freshly baked bannock are far better than sliced bread. Snacks that contain fat, like fruitcake, work well, so you're not

Who invited the black-capped chickadee for supper?

biting into something frozen solid all the time. Dry treats like shortbread don't freeze and are good choices. Place a sheet of waxed paper between your sandwiches so they don't become one solid lump.

Camp stoves

If I'm hot tenting, I use the wood stove. If cold camping, I prefer to keep the campfire for warmth and being social with my camping companions and limit the cooking to a camp stove. It gets the meal cooked quicker. However, a campfire does have some advantages over a stove when it comes to baking, frying up bacon or grilling up a steak. It's best to start cooking after the embers have burned down, and control the heat by piling up the coals to heat it up or spreading them apart to cool it down. A blanket of ash covering the coals as an insulator controls the heat better for cooking, especially when cooking things like potatoes, corn or onions wrapped in tin foil.

There are lots of camp stove models and fuel types available out there. That's the problem — there are too many to choose from. You've got your two burners and single burners.

You've got gas-fueled, liquid-fueled and multi-fueled. There are stoves that need to be primed and some that switch on by an electronic ignition. You even have some stoves that cost a small fortune and some homemade versions that can be made out of a tuna can and a piece of cardboard.

Here's a general breakdown to help you decide on which ones to purchase, based mainly on fuel types and boiling times.

Butane/propane

Canister stoves are one of the preferred designs for campers. It is a clean-burning, reliable, and trouble-free stove which operates on a pressurized canister (butane/propane) that is attached to the stove and punctured to let loose the vaporized gas. The flame can be controlled easily and placed at a simmer, unlike many of the other stove

Jetboil makes a great lightweight and effective butane stove.

BUTANE/PROPANE STOVE TIPS

To help fix the problem with some butane/propane stoves not working well in cold temperatures:

- Warm the cylinder up by placing it under your armpit for a few minutes or rubbing it in your palms. Storing it in your sleeping bag during the night can also be a plus. If frost forms on the canister itself, stand it in a dish of water and agitate the water slightly. This will stop the canister from cooling below 32°F (0°C).
- Try to boil when the canister is full and simmer when it's nearly empty. The full canister has greater mass so the cooling of the liquefied gas is less of a problem. And the close-to-empty canister doesn't put out enough gas while simmering, so cooling isn't such an issue.
- If at all possible, attempt boiling small amounts of water at one time. The stove will then only push to peak output for a few minutes and not allow enough time for the liquid gas in the canister to cool down.
- Wind is just much an issue with canister stoves as it is with white gas. However, watch that the windshield is tall enough to protect the entire stove but doesn't allow the canister to heat up.
- Integrated stove systems (i.e., the Jetboil) are far more fuel-efficient in the cold. The stove is attached directly to the cooking pot, resulting in an improved transfer of heat from the burner to the pot and a dramatic increase in boil times.

The best part of the Trangia stove is that not much can go wrong with it. It's like a fancy fondue set.

models. It also sells at a good price. The gas contained in the canister is a blend of propane and either butane or iso-butane. Why a blended gas? Butane is more stable than propane at varying temperatures and allows for safer storage in such a small, lightweight container. Also, butane doesn't work well in cold temperatures, but propane does. The added propane will boost the performance while winter camping. Take note: if the canister is too cold the propane will quickly burn off, leaving you with a canister of slow-burning butane.

Alcohol

It's not that easy to find alcohol stoves anymore in North America. The stove does have some disadvantages, one being too short a burning time to cook an entire meal without refueling. It also has the added danger of having to reach into the stove, slide a metal disc over the burner, and adjust a flame you can hardly see. Alcohol burns

HOW MUCH FUEL DO I BRING ALONG?

The amount of fuel needed has so many variables: fuel type, the air temperature, wind and the design of a windscreen used, maximum heat output (BTU) of the stove, even the type of pots and pans used. Overall, however, the best way to judge your fuel consumption is to plan 40 minutes of cooking time for dinner and 20 minutes for preparing a hot breakfast. Let's say you're going on a five-day trip. That adds up to four dinners (two hours and 40 minutes of burning time) and four breakfasts (one hour and 10 minutes). Now add an extra hour for a couple of hot soups for lunch or an extreme cold weather snap that will rob you of extra fuel. So, to be on the safe side, you can say you need a little more than five hours of fuel for a five-day trip. If your stove runs on white gas, and burns quick and hot like the MSR models, with a pump/fuel bottle, it will use up 1 quart (1 L) bottle of fuel every three days, which means you bring 2 quarts (2 L) for five days to be on the safe side. If you have butane/propane stoves which run on pressurized canisters, then two canisters should be enough, with a little to spare.

An organized kitchen area and a hearty meal warms the toes of any winter camper.

clean and colorless.

The positive points of the stove excel over the negative, however. First, it's extremely lightweight. It fits in the palm of your hand. It also can come with its own cook set and is quite compact. I pack mine as a backup with my stick stove (a stove that's fueled by small twigs) in case of wet weather. They're also very simple — what I mean is, there's nothing much to them and nothing much can go wrong with them. It's like a mini fondue set. And most of all, they're unbelievably silent. No pressurized gas is needed.

White gas

White gas is a good winter camping choice. The stove models are more expensive than most other fuel-type designs. However, since white gas is relatively cheap to buy, and there are no separate cylinders to purchase, they are actually less expensive in the long run. White gas stoves also require priming, which can be a real hassle, but they're also far more efficient in cold temperatures. For most models, it's possible to spend extra and have them burn more than one type of fuel (i.e., unleaded gas, kerosene, diesel,

An MSR Dragonfly white gas stove: one of the best options for cooking in cold temperatures.

MAINTAINING YOUR WHITE GAS STOVE

- Only fill the fuel container to three-quarters. No pressure can be created if it's full, and the stove will refuse to light properly.
- Make sure to oil or replace the rubber gaskets inside the pressure cap at least once a season. After continual use, the gaskets have a tendency to break down and leak. To check for leakage, squirt a drop of liquid detergent around the pressure cap. If bubbles form, you have a problem.
- Make sure to pack replacement parts and a mini-tool kit for the stove. To help familiarize yourself with your stove, as well as to help you fix it when the darn thing breaks down, it helps to take the stove completely apart and back together again prior to your trip.
- Some models may need priming paste to help lighting in cold temperatures.

jet fuel). However, unless you're going to countries where white gas is unavailable, it's a waste of money. Also, wind can rob the stove of unbelievable amounts of fuel. Make sure to place an aluminum windscreen around and under the stove. Even on warm, windless days, the screen will cook up dinner far quicker.

Take note that liquid gas can quickly become the same temperature as the air, and you can easily get frostbite if you spill it on your bare skin in freezing temperatures.

Reducing flare-ups: A flare-up, which only happens on stoves fueled by white gas, is a large yellow flame that forces everyone in camp to run for cover while the stove operator fiddles with the control to reduce it to a much safer, stunted blue flame. This occurs when liquid gas exits the stove while the burner is cold. To maintain control on stoves like the MSR WhisperLite or DragonFly, make sure to place enough fuel in the priming cup and check that it has almost burnt away, to properly preheat the burner, before turning the switch to on. Stoves that have no priming cup are ignited by spraying a mixture of air and gas into the chamber below the burner, ready to be set alight. To have the mixture properly exit the stove, you must pump up the stove enough

It seems there's an overwhelming number of stove options out there. Just remember, the simpler the better. Photo: Colin Angus

to create pressure to form the spray. If it's not pumped enough, then liquid fuel leaks into the chamber and floods it, flaring up until the extra fuel burns off. Once the flame calms down, the stove's pressure must be pumped back up before a second attempt is made.

Stick stoves

It makes a lot of sense for winter campers to use "stick stoves" rather than the common butane/propane, alcohol or white gas stoves. Stick stoves are fueled by small twigs and forest debris (i.e., pine cones, bark). They're definitely not new to the outdoor

scene, and it seems a lot more campers are switching away from petroleum-based stoves to natural forest fibers. They're simple, dependable, environmentally friendly and, above all, genuine.

These nine are the best of the lot:

Littlbug: This is a stick stove that continually receives great reviews. It's compact, but strong and stable enough to support large pots — even my cast-iron Dutch oven. Perfect for winter hot-tenting excursions. It's made of durable stainless steel and it has a very simple design. It forms a half-moon shape

Stick stoves are a huge bonus on winter trips. My preference is the Kelly Kettle stove.

when stored away and fits around a sleeping bag stored in my pack.

There's no battery-powered blower, but vent holes in the windscreen allow enough air circulation to keep the flames going strong. As an added bonus, much like other newer stick stoves, a Trangia alcohol stove nests perfectly inside the windscreen to be used as a backup in case of wet weather or lack of forest debris.

There's a Senior Littlbug 3 pounds (1.4 kg) and Junior ½-pound (200 g). The Junior is for the lightweight backpacking crowd or solo camper. The only downfall is its assembly process. It's simple once you figure it out, but the initial setup is like figuring out a Rubik's Cube for the first time.

Firebox: I'm impressed with the amount of heat this stove puts out. The Firebox has good airflow and a pot of water reaches a boil just as quick as, or even quicker than, on a regular gas stove. It packs away nicely and the size and design allows for various dimensions of pots to sit on top — it even comes with a grill so you can cook a juicy steak. A Trangia alcohol stove fits snugly inside as well.

There are a few disadvantages. The weight is a hefty 2 pounds (900 g). This is fine if you're hauling gear on a sled, but nearly one kilogram of stainless steel is a burden when backpacking. However, Firebox has a smaller and lighter version, weighing only about 6 ounces (170 g).

Emberlit FireAnt Stove: If you're looking for the lightest and most compact stick stove out there, this is it. Made of titanium, it comes in at only 80 grams. The entire stove packs flat, to the thickness of a piece of newsprint. Amazing! When put together, it measures just 3 ½" x 5" (9 x 13 cm). Surprisingly, it's also steady. It consists of four walls and two accessories: a base plate and a small shelf. The shelf attaches to the upper portion of the stove and holds Esbit solid fuel tablets. The stove also comes equipped with slots that hold a Trangia alcohol stove.

Kelly Kettle Hobo Stove: What sets the Kelly Kettle apart from all other stick stoves is its ingenious double-wall chimney. After lighting your debris (or any other combustible material) in the base plate, the flames are drawn upward through a fire chamber, reacting like a chimney draft. The water is stored in a water jacket that surrounds the chimney, which enables the stove to rapidly boil water, even in wet and windy weather conditions.

The Kelly Kettle has one disadvantage — it's bulky at 21 ounces (600 g) or more. An aluminum model can replace the standard stainless-steel unit, to lighten things up. I pack the smaller Trekker model on most canoe trips and use the Base Camp model for trips when there are more people in the group. The company also has the Hobo Stove. The base can be used as a stand-alone stick stove and is much easier to cook up a full meal on.

VitalGrill Survival Stove: This stove hit the market a dozen years ago or so. The original intent was to sell it to doomsday preppers, not to backwoods campers. However, campers gravitated more towards this stove than Armageddon worshippers did… and that's a good thing.

The VitalGrill works on the same principle as most stick stoves. It burns any material found around the forest floor and uses that heat to cook a meal or boil a pot of water. It does separate itself from the crowd, however, with its battery-operated blower.

Having a fan constantly feeding the flames allows this stove to produce as much as 20,000 BTU, reaching 1200°F (650°C). A mechanical shutter can adjust the airflow as well, making it hotter or cooler, just like a flue on a woodstove. The VitalGrill is heavy — weighing 26 ounces (740 g) — and if you run out of batteries you'll end up carrying an ineffective and bulky fire box.

BioLite: Like many of the stick stove designs out there, crowd-sourcing created the BioLite. And buyers loved it. The BioLite has all the advantages of a stick stove, plus an electric blower fan that is powered by the heat generated from burning fuel. Brilliant! It can even use (and store) excess energy to charge electronics, like your iPhone.

The BioLite rang true to all the hype when it was introduced a few years back. It burns well, gets water boiling as fast as a gas stove and it creates its own energy. It's not the lightest or smallest stove, however, at 33 ounces (935 g) and the size of a Nalgene water bottle. Charging an iPhone also takes a lot of burn time. I boiled two liters of water and only gained a 10 percent charge.

180 Stove: This is another robust stick stove. It's a bit heavy, weighing 10 ounces (285 g), but is still very compact. There are no moving parts, hinges or rivets. The large cooking surface 6" x 7" (15 x 17 cm) is a real bonus. However, the biggest advantage over all the other designs is that the three sidewalls act as a windscreen and allow ample room to feed in fuel.

KIHD Stove: This is a newer design and is made of cold rolled steel, weighing in at 23 ounces (640 g). The bonus is that this stove comes with a door which greatly helps to control your flames while cooking. It's fairly easy to set up and comes with an extra set of cross straps to mount your cooking pot on. The stove can be used with wood sticks, wood chunks, charcoal briquettes and fuel pods. A Trangia stove fits perfectly inside it as well.

Bushbuddy Stove: This stove is different. It's a wood gasifier, which means it has a double-walled combustion chamber for a clean and intense burn. Air heats in the space between the walls, and is drawn into the top of the chamber towards the smoke and gases. This creates an almost smokeless fire. You light the fire inside the chamber and continue to add wood and sticks. It's so fuel efficient. It also has a solid heat shield to reduce scorching what its set on. The only disadvantage is its hefty price.

Camp kitchen

You can set up a perfect camp kitchen while cold-weather camping. Use a small packable shovel or your snowshoes to dig a 3-foot-deep (1 m) trench in the snow. From there you can carve out a table, chairs, storage and cooking area. The area provides shelter from the wind, helping to save fuel in your camp stove.

Stainless-steel pots and pans (or cast iron if you don't have to carry them far) are the way to go. Aluminum is

Freshly caught and fried fish served with a pot of mac and cheese. Yum!

lighter and cheaper, but doesn't do as good a job. A 3-quart (3 L) pot with a 2-quart (2 L) pot nestled inside is sufficient for two to four people. More than that and you'd better go with an 8-quart (8 L) pot with a 4- or 6-quart (4 or 6 L) one nestled inside.

Some campers think it's an absolute sin to use pots over a campfire rather than a cook stove due to them getting blackened by the soot from the fire. Others believe the charcoal color adds character and even adds flavor to the food. If you follow the second

philosophy, then just make sure to store the pot set in a separate storage bag and pack a pair of cooking gloves. Coating the outside of the pot with soap also helps minimize the amount of soot collected.

Extreme lightweight campers use a pot lid as a frying pan. It's the handle of the frying pan that makes it difficult to pack, so either remove the handle from the pan after you buy it or simply buy one without a handle — just make sure to take a pot-gripper. A griddle can also be used when cooking for larger groups — perfect for a couple rows of flapjacks surrounded by bacon. Combine the griddle with a firebox or campfire grill and you can make some amazing meals for large groups.

You'll need a knife, fork and spoon for each person. A spork (half fork and half spoon) can help reduce weight and bulk. Extra utensils that come in handy include a whisk, cheese grater, large spoon and a spatula. Buy mini versions of these utensils when you see them at stores or garage sales.

Campers usually prefer plastic plates. However, there are all sorts of specialized lightweight choices out there. A Frisbee isn't a bad idea. It can be used to hold a paper plate, which is burned in the fire after use. The Frisbee can be tossed around camp as well. Drinking mugs can be enamel or stainless steel, but an insulated mug is far handier. A good rule to follow is to make sure that your mugs will fit snugly inside your pot set.

Today there is a huge assortment of reusable containers available to store spices and foods. Various sizes of wide-mouth polyethylene bottles are great. So are plastic vitamin bottles. But make sure to double-pack everything in zipper storage bags, just in case. Christina Scheuermann shares her own method for beating the cold: "I keep a lighter tucked in my sports bra. Always works when the fluid in others freezes up!"

Water treatment

Water filters are the easiest piece of camp gear to eliminate parasites. The trouble is, they freeze up in the winter and become useless. You still must treat your water, however, mostly due to a tiny parasite called *Giardia lamblia*. It's deposited in the water by the feces of infected animals. The usual host is the beaver, hence the term "beaver fever," but it can be deposited by any mammal, including humans.

It only takes ten *Giardia* cysts to infect your body. The microscopic protozoan, measuring 21 microns in length (the tip of a sewing needle measures 700 microns), hatches inside the small intestine with an incubation period from five days to several months, reproduces like wildfire, establishes a colony, and then has a little party in your gut — making you feel as if Montezuma has moved north to seek his revenge.

Symptoms can be severe or completely unnoticeable. They include diarrhea, abdominal cramps, fatigue,

Frozen water all around you, free for the gathering.

weight loss, flatulence, and nausea — not a pleasant experience while being away from flush toilets and a local pharmacy. Usually, however, you get it when at home and then just assume it's the flu. However, if the parasite does not get treated, it can cause severe problems. I've been affected three times and each case took over a month to treat with antibiotics.

Giardia is the most common pathogen to find swimming around in your water bottle. The good news, however, is that it's the least dangerous. The protozoa *Francisella tularensis* is a little more serious. Tularemia is similar to an infectious plague-like disease that infects man and more than eighty percent of other species of mammals.

It is also caused by a bacterium, which gains entrance to the body and multiplies rapidly through the bloodstream, invading cells of the liver, spleen, lungs, kidneys, and lymph nodes.

When a person is infected by tularemia they can expect the worst flu-like symptoms: a high temperature, headaches, chills, sweat, nausea, vomiting, and body pain. Extreme symptoms, as if the others aren't bad enough, are: a swollen area where the infection entered (hands, arm, face or neck), inflammation of eye membrane, and general enlargement of the lymph nodes.

The parasitic protozoa can be transmitted the same way as *Giardia* — ingestion of water contaminated by either the feces or the carcass of an infected mammal. It can also be given by inoculation from biting insects (bloodsucking flies, ticks, lice, or fleas). A very high number of trappers fall ill to this sickness due to their constant contact with the internal organs and body fluids of mammals.

Apart from the pathogens, *Giardia* and tularemia, there are many varieties of bacteria floating around in the water supply as well. *E. coli* gives you a nasty case of the trots. *Kleisiella pneumoniae* causes pneumonia, and *Salmonella* can give you either a bad case of food poisoning or a bout of typhoid fever. Then there are surface-water pollutants like gas fuel, pesticides, and heavy metals from old mine sites — all of which gives you a good reason to treat all water while you're out there.

Boiling

Boiling water in the summer months to treat it is the less common technique. It's time-consuming and uses too much fuel. Boiling in the winter is commonplace, however. Having the water boil for five minutes will eliminate most of everything, and just having it come to a rolling boil is sufficient to get rid of protozoa, bacteria and even viruses.

Chemical treatment

Iodine tablets or any other form of chemical treatment is another option for cleaning water. The chemical works well in killing most of what's out there. It should be noted, however, that there's a strong odor, not to mention a bland taste to the water. Just remember that it takes time to let the water sit before it's drinkable, and it has an odd taste as well.

Melted snow makes terrible tea

Melted snow has a weird taste to it, something between overdone toast and burnt milk. If you have to melt snow for water, then add a bit of water in the pot first. That reduces the bad taste, but doesn't eliminate it. Melting snow also wastes valuable fuel, and you'll need handfuls of it to make a single cup of water. If you're lucky, really lucky, you'll be camped beside an open section of water near a running stream. Or a layer of slush is covering the lake you've camped beside. It's more common, however, to cut a hole in the ice to gather fresh water. An ice auger is the quickest way through. It's bulky and heavy, though.

The best augers are the fold-up models, with an extension shaft if the ice is extra-thick. Generally, it should go through at least 3 feet (1 m) of ice without using the extension. A dull auger blade makes it a real chore. Keep your blades sharp. They become close to useless if you hit a rock while going through the ice. Just make sure to

Fresh water makes better tea than melted snow. Pack an ice auger, above left, or a traditional ice chisel, above right.

keep the blade guard on: a new blade is crazy razor-sharp.

An ice chisel is more traditional and, when used properly, becomes a very efficient way to retrieve water. The chisel is a heavy steel blade (beveled on one side is best) with a steel sleeve in which to fit a long wooden pole, which is, in turn, held in place by a screw. A leash is attached to it and your forearm to make sure you don't lose it down the ice hole.

You carry the chisel with you, which is attached to the elongated pole when you get to camp. It takes time, patience and skill to use the well-sharpened chisel to cut through to open water. It's a skill you either wear with pride or something you end up despising.

My group of winter campers play a game of paper, rock, scissors to choose who's going down to the lake to chisel the hole. I've lost more often than not. It's not bad once you get the hang of it, though. Sometimes it's even a nice peaceful time, hard labor mixed with tranquility.

How to keep water from freezing

Use an insulated container (thermos) to store water while traveling, or buy/ build an insulated bottle holder. To keep your water from freezing overnight, store the thermos inside your sleeping bag or place it outside, in a snow bank, upside-down so if it does begin to freeze the ice will be at the bottom of the container. The snow should insulate it enough to keep it from freezing solid, however. (Just make sure to mark the spot where you've buried it.) And remember: placing juice crystals in your water will will freeze at lower temperatures than pure water — so suit it up if you like.

Dehydrating foods

Dehydrated meals are lighter and more compact than fresh or canned food, perfect for longer winter treks or campers who are backpacking rather than hauling their gear on a toboggan. Drying food is definitely not new. The process of dehydrating predates recorded history. Drying fruit (plums become prunes, grapes raisins, and figs dates) goes back before Biblical times. Dried cod was the main food source across Europe over 500 years ago. The voyageurs lived off of pemmican, made up of dried meat with dried berries mixed into it. NASA used the process of dehydration to feed the first astronauts bite-sized cubed meals during their first trip to the moon.

There are a number of drying processes. Open air, the sun, smoke or the wind were the most common methods before technology kicked into gear. Now solar or electric food dehydrators speed up the process and keep

Dehydrating Mexican stew — delicious and lightweight. Photo: Cobi Sharpe

TURKEY JERKY

You'll be surprised at how easy it is to make your own jerky. Start off with purchasing meats with the least fat. A round roast or chicken works well — even tofu can be done — but by far the best is turkey. Slice the meat across the grain and marinate for two to four hours in ½ cup (125 ml) Worcestershire sauce, ½ cup (125 ml) soy sauce and ¼ cup (60 ml) red wine vinegar. Then lay the slices across the oven racks and dry overnight (8 to 12 hours) at 150°F (65°C). If it snaps in half when bent, it's done. You can simply snack on it or add it to soups or stews.

things more consistent. There's also the method of freeze-drying, whereby food is frozen and water is then removed by sublimation.

Drying your own food is by far the best way to prepare camp meals. It's not as if those prepackaged dehydrated meals aren't palatable or wholesome. We've come a long way from breakfasts of green powered eggs and dinners of mock-shepherd's pie that tastes like biting into cardboard. But there's so much more to experimenting and making your own meals. It's also a lot less expensive (and fun) to try it on your own.

You can pick up a good dehydrator for less than $100, but you can also place items on racks in your oven and use a cookie sheet, coated with a layer of cooking oil, to dehydrate sauces. Set the oven at the lowest temperature possible and leave for six to eight hours. You also might want to use a toothpick to keep the door open a little to help keep the air circulating, especially if you have a gas stove. The stove is perfect for sauces and meats, but may be too hot to properly prepare fruits and vegetables. It depends on the stove.

Sauces are the best thing to practice on. One jar of spaghetti sauce placed in the dehydrator or oven is reduced to a thin slice of what looks like fruit leather. Then, once at camp, you simply place the dried sauce in a small amount of boiling water (about ½ cup/125 ml), and it turns right back into the original spaghetti sauce.

Vegetables are also quite easy to dehydrate. It's a good idea to spend the winter months buying up different veggies on sale and then drying them in bulk for use later on. Some favorites are broccoli, celery, green and red peppers, mushrooms, zucchini, corn, peas and eggplant.

Meat takes a lot more preparation. It first must be cooked before drying. Some meats, such as cooked ground beef, should also be rinsed over and over again with hot water to eliminate the grease content and reduce the chances of bacteria forming. Drying ground turkey or ground venison is an amazing way to add substance to a camp meal. It has less fat and therefore less chance of spoiling while you are out on the trip.

Take note, however, that some dried foods are best bought directly at the bulk food store. Onions and garlic really stink up the house when dried in the dehydrator, and banana chips and pineapple slices look less appetizing done at home than the ones you can pick up at the bulk food store. Dipping some fruit like apple slices in lemon juice reduces the bruised coloring. Also, if you slice the food too thickly it won't fully dehydrate, and if you slice it too thinly it will crumble in the storage bag. It's also not a good idea to dehydrate strong-smelling foods (i.e., mushrooms, asparagus) with other foods if you don't want everything smelling the same. Some

fruits (blueberries, cherries) should be pierced with a toothpick prior to drying to drain juice and speed up the drying process. Vegetables that you generally don't eat raw should also be blanched first, boiling them in water or steaming them. This scalding action destroys naturally-occurring enzymes that contribute to flavor loss, texture change and color change during storage.

If you're going to invest in a food dehydrator, then make sure it has a fan. If not, the process takes way too long. A thermostat is also a bonus. The trays work better if they're round, not square, which ensures better airflow and temperature distribution. The top and bottom should also be insulated to reduce heat loss. And make sure you can add or reduce trays, and that the product comes with a tray for sauces and finer mess trays for drying smaller items (i.e., corn, peas, olives). If not, you could line the main tray with waxed paper or parchment paper.

Adult beverages

Cowboy coffee

True camp coffee is nothing but real grounds-and-water-in-the-pot coffee. Bring water to a rolling boil, take it off the heat source, dump in one generous tablespoon of coffee grounds per

cup of water, and let it steep (covered) alongside the campfire for approximately five to 10 minutes. To settle the grounds, tap a spoon on the side of the pot three to five times.

The most crucial element of brewing

Dave Marrone brews up cowboy coffee, using centrifugal force to push the grounds to the bottom of the pot.

"true grit" is to never let the coffee boil once you've taken it off the heat source. Old-timers used to say that boiled coffee tastes like rotten shoe leather, and they're right! The reason for the bad taste of boiled coffee is in the bitter tannic acid and flavouring oils it contains. The tasty oils are released at 187°F (86°C), just below boiling point. The bitter acids, however, are released right at or just above boiling pot.

Another important factor is how to settle the grounds before serving the coffee. Some campers throw pieces of eggshell or toss in a few round pebbles. A teaspoon of cold water seems to do the trick as well, or simply tapping the side of the pot three or four times with a knife or spoon. The classic way, however, is to believe in the physics of centrifugal force. Take a hold of the wire handle on the pot, swing it with the speed of an aircraft propeller, and have complete faith that the quick motion will force the grounds to the bottom of the pot and keep the boiled water from spilling out on top of you. This suicidal action isn't as effective as all the other options, but campmates will be more impressed with it. Just make sure to give the person in the group you don't necessarily like the first cup of coffee and the last, where all the grounds are still floating freely about. And the last touch is a healthy dash of sweet-smelling Irish Cream liqueur.

Single malt scotch whisky

There are campers out there that truly believe that the only spirit that should be packed along on a trip is a single malt whisky. Tradition states that only two ounces after dinner, preferably with a cigar, is all that's required on trip. The only bulky part is the container holding it and the glass you're drinking from. It's supposedly a sin to use anything but glass. Scotch stored in a Nalgene water bottle and sipped from an enamel camp mug is definitely frowned upon — but it's still certainly doable.

To make it last a little longer, it's quite acceptable to add a bit of water. The flavor of Scotch brands is varied and most take time to acquire a taste for. Ten-year-old Talisker from the Isle of Skye is a great choice. Highland Park from Orkney Islands, northern Scotland, is the most economical libation in its class and was the source of many Hudson Bay Company employees. Whatever the brand, make sure to give scotch a try on your next trip. After all, with so many outdoor enthusiasts glorifying it so much, it's got to have some magical quality about it.

Winter teas

Pine tea

White pine needles contain vitamins A, B_1, B_2, B_3, calcium, iron, phosphorus, potassium, and sodium. They also contain polyprenols, physterols and carotenoids, making a mighty antioxidant brew.

White pine tea served with a splash of rum and brown sugar.

Spruce tea

White and black spruce needles have a high vitamin C, beta carotene, starch, and sugar count. They're harsh-tasting, though, and not one of my favorites in the winter. I prefer the new tips in late spring.

Balsam fir tea

Balsam fir has vitamins C, B_1, B_2, B_3, calcium, iron, phosphorus, potassium, sodium, beta carotene, protein and fiber. It makes a good and nutritious broth.

Yellow birch tea

My all-time favorite. Small twigs boiled up have a strong winter green taste. It also contains vitamins B_1, B_2, calcium, iron, magnesium, manganese and zinc. White birch contains betulinol, glycosides, flavonoids, saponins,

Chaga fungal growth makes a delicious and healthy tea. Photo: Claire Quewezence

Labrador tea

This is the tea of the North. It's found in sphagnum swamps across the northern United States and Canada. The leaves are dried and boiled. To cut the strong acidic taste, try adding a spoon of brown sugar and a shot of liqueur. The leaves stay on all winter long.

Wild rose

The fruit (rosehip) of the plant is the best part and hangs on the plant through the winter. It can be eaten raw or dried for later use. Only eat the outer shell of the rosehip and not the hairy seed cluster.

Nature's winter bounty is everywhere — take a look at the wild rose hip.

sesquiterpenes, and tannins, but has a very bland taste. Research shows that birch bark contains xylitol, which kills bacteria and reduces cavities. Maybe chewing on a twig throughout the day isn't a bad idea

Chaga tea

Chaga is a fungal growth that grows on mature birch trees and is an amazing find if you spot it. It fights cancer, helps the immune system, aids the digestion system, acts as a longevity tonic, a DNA-shielding agent, and reduces stress. It also makes a nice strong tea. Best when dried first and chopped up into a powder.

The comforts of life's essentials —
food, fire, and friendships...
—Julia Child

CHAPTER 7

Baking in the Bush

THERE'S NO EXCUSE TO AVOID baking fresh bread, or anything else for that matter, while camping out. Reflector ovens are great to pack on a trip; Dutch ovens have become commonplace in many outdoor kitchen sets; and a product called the Outback Oven has revolutionized the process of baking up brownies, cakes and pies.

Outback Ovens are a lightweight baking system that can be used with pressurized-gas camp stoves. The main component is the heat diffuser at the base, which allows the heat to be evenly distributed. A hood — resembling a tea cozy — is then placed over the Teflon-coated pan. Just make sure to use a stove model that can simmer or at least puts out an even heat. If not, you'll have a lot of burnt food. Also, make sure that the gas cylinder is separate and away from the burner. If not, the hood, when placed over the pot and stove, will heat up the pressurized gas cylinder and it may explode.

Making use of a reflector oven can dramatically alter a trip. It's not a necessary piece of kitchen gear by any means, but once you try it out, you'll never go on a camping trip without one. The benefits definitely make up for the weight and bulk. Imagine fresh bread, pita pizza, blueberry pie, brownies or muffins. The ovens are made of either lightweight aluminum or stainless steel and are concave in design. Placing the oven beside the campfire reflects the radiant heat inside and evenly bakes whatever is on the wire rack. The angle has to be watched now and then to moderate the amount of heat, and it's best to wait so there's a good bed of coals before you start baking. The better models fold down to fit inside a pack.

The reflector oven takes a lot longer to bake in colder temperatures, and baking is a little more complicated of an affair than pan-frying bannock. It takes up a lot of time and fuel. But the sight of a loaf's golden-brown top is heavenly, and the sweet smell given off when the first slice has been handed out is pure bliss. But doubly so on a cold, winter's day.

Dutch oven camp cooking

I make every dinner with a Dutch Oven while hot tenting in winter.

One of the best ways to cook a delicious meal while out camping is to use the traditional Dutch oven. It seems everyone that's tried it are die-hard fans. However, campers that haven't cooked a meal with one generally question if it's worth the weight and bulk.

I generally use my Dutch oven during winter camping trips. Packing it on the freight toboggan doesn't seem so bad compared to a canoe pack.

The Dutch oven originated in Holland around the early 1700s and has been widely used around the world

110

ever since. George Washington fed his troops with it, and Lewis and Clark cooked up horse stew on their historic trek to the West Coast. It was used to cook bake beans during the cattle drives and sourdough bread during the Klondike gold rush. Military camps used it during World War 1, and by the 1970s, it had become one of the top choices for campers to cook a meal.

So why the popularity? After all, it's heavy and bulky. The answer is simple — whatever is cooked in it tastes fantastic. And it cooks just about everything.

The Dutch oven also refers to the following: a camp oven, an outdoor oven, a kitchen oven and a bean pot. The bean pot and kitchen oven are basically the same design, equipped with a rounded lid, flat bottom and no legs. These are generally used at home and in the oven. The camp oven and outdoor oven are a different style, with a flanged lid, a flat bottom with three legs and a steel bail handle for carrying. This is the style used for camping, with the flanged lid designed for holding hot coals and the legs used to hold the pot above the campfire embers.

Dutch ovens are commonly made from cast iron. The material distributes heat evenly and retains heat, which is why the oven is so effective. The solid lid seals the pot and steams the contents, which keeps in the moisture and the food tender. Cast iron is also long lasting and can be passed down from generation to generation.

To cut down in weight, there are aluminum Dutch ovens available. This is an added bonus for anyone who wants to pack it along on an interior trip. Many traditionalists slam the use of the aluminum, but the weight difference is significant — cast iron weighs in at 18 pounds and an aluminum model weighs a mere 7 pounds. Aluminum also doesn't rust and can be washed easily with soap and water. Some models come with a non-stick coating. Aluminum also doesn't discolor the food like cast iron. The pot heats up quicker as well. This can be more of a disadvantage, however. The heat has a tendency to fluctuate too much, making it far easier to burn your meal in an aluminum oven than a cast iron one.

Dutch oven care

Whichever one you decide to purchase, make sure the lid fits to create a good seal but can be moved slightly from side to side. If it's a cast iron model, then give it a good wash with soap, water and a scrub brush. Most cast iron manufacturers place an edible protective wax coating to stop it from rusting during shipment. Right after you wash the Dutch oven, it's time to season it with vegetable shortening. After this point, soap is never to be used while

A balsam or spruce bough makes a great pot scrubber.

washing the Dutch oven. The oven must be continually seasoned. Cast iron is incredibly porous, like a sponge, and the cooking oil fills the fine holes. Aluminum ovens also benefit from the seasoning process, even though aluminum doesn't rust like iron, but it does oxidize. A layer of oil will prevent that from happening.

Rub the shortening on the entire surface of the cast iron. Then, heat it up in your kitchen oven or your outside barbecue or a campfire. The seasoning step is a stinky and smoky job (but an important process), so you're best choosing the outside options. Oil is continually added throughout the use of the oven and eventually you'll create a non-stick surface.

BAKING WITH A WOOD STOVE
A reflector oven leaned up against the side of the stove does a fine job for cookies and cinnamon rolls. The bottoms will need a little direct heat by placing the pan on top for a while. I alternate between the stove top and the oven to get an even bake.
— Rhonda Reynolds

Dutch oven recipes

Breakfast Cornbread

Cooking cornbread in a Dutch oven while sipping on morning coffee and stoking the wood stove inside a cozy canvas tent has to be one of the greatest joys while winter camping. Of course, you might have to substitute the pancake syrup with some dark rum if the cold temperature freezes the syrup. Egg powder doesn't freeze solid like an egg at -20°C as well.

2 tbsp granulated sugar
¼ tsp each ground ginger, cinnamon
    and nutmeg
2 cups milk
¼ cup cornmeal
1 egg
¼ cup pancake syrup

At home: Combine sugar, ginger, cinnamon and nutmeg. Store in a small sealed plastic bag.

At camp: Heat milk in a saucepan. Stir in the cornmeal; reduce heat and simmer, stirring frequently until thickened. Remove from heat. Combine oil and egg, stir into cornmeal mixture. Add sugar and spice mixture and syrup. Spoon into an 8 inch (20 cm) lightly greased metal pan. Place in the Dutch oven. Cook for 40 minutes or

CAMPING TIP
This bread will need to be cooked with coals both on top of and under the Dutch oven.

until bread is lightly browned and firm to the touch.

Sweet Potato & Black Bean Quinoa Chili

A tasty, nutritious and light-weight veggie chili that really hits the spot.

1-2 sweet potato, sliced
1 medium red onion, sliced
1 avocado
1 dehydrated red peppers
3 garlic cloves
1 cup black beans
1-2 dehydrated tomatoes
1 vegetable broth cube
1 can dehydrated tomato paste
½ cup quinoa
1– 1 ½ tablespoons chili powder
2 tsp cumin
2 tsp paprika
1 tsp coriander
½ tsp cayenne

Add all ingredients to Dutch oven. Cover and cook for 2 hours. Uncover and top with slices avocado.

No-Knead Garlic Rosemary Bread

Adding this to a meal is a quick and easy way to wow other campers. Just don't let them know how uncomplicated the recipe really is. It's best to always keep them guessing. On guided trips, I'd serve these slices with reconstituted dehydrated salsa sauce and pair them with a crisp Sauvignon Blanc.

3 ½ cups all-purpose flour
1 package of rapid rise yeast
1 tsp coarse sea salt
1 ½ cups warm water
1 tablespoon dried rosemary
1-2 garlic glove

Roast the garlic gloves by cutting the tops off, wrapping them in tinfoil and cooking on hot coals until golden brown. Mix the other ingredients and half the roasted garlic, in a bowl. Cover and let sit for a few hours. Coat your hands in cooking oil and push the dough down. Place the dough onto floured parchment paper, sprinkle the top with dried rosemary and the rest of the chopped up roasted garlic. Cook in the Dutch oven for 30-35 minutes. Remove the cover and bake for another 10 minutes until golden brown.

Stout Stew

I've made a lot of stews while out winter camping, but this has to be my pride and joy recipe.

4 lbs cubed beef
½ flour
1 tall-can stout Beer (Guinness is good)
½ cup red wine
1 ½ cups good beef stock.
1 tsp nutmeg
1 tsp cracked black pepper
2 sprigs chopped fresh rosemary
1 tbsp fresh thyme
2 cloves chopped garlic
2 small red onions, minced
2-4 carrots, chopped

2-4 parsnip, chopped
1 lb turnip, cut in large chunks
1 medium pearl onion
4-6 baby red potatoes
salt and pepper

Season beef in salt and pepper, then cover in flour and brown in an oiled Dutch oven. Place cooked beef in Dutch oven and add the rest of the ingredients, using a quarter to a half tall-can of the stout. Cook for 2 hours.

Mom's Fruitcake

My mother, born in Scotland, would put a slice of fruitcake in our Christmas stockings each year. My sisters routinely found places to hide it. They hated fruit cake. I loved it and would search out their stashes. Now I don't go on a winter trip without some stored in my pack.No search necessary!

Fruit cake has gotten a bad rap for quite some time. It was once a cherished treat back in the 18th and 19th centuries when ingredients were rare and expensive. That's why my mother started placing it in our Christmas stockings. Somewhere down the line,

however, it became commonplace to hate it. There's even an annual fruitcake toss where people in Colorado hurl unwanted cake with medieval catapults.

Fruitcake has been around for a long time. The ancient Romans mixed barley, pomegranate seeds, nuts and raisins — creating some sort of energy bar. German Christmas bread, called "stolen," and the Italian holiday bread, known as "panettone," are other close kin for the fruitcake. So is Russian Easter bread, known as "kulich" and Irish fruit bread, which is called "barmbrack." English Fruitcake, or what Canadians call "Christmas cake," peaked during Victorian times. Fruit was a rarity in winter, and fruitcake contained dried sugary portions. It was also soaked in brandy well before the holidays began. Winter campers, however, would appreciate why the ancient Egyptians made fruitcake and placed it with the bodies of their departed loved ones to carry with them to the afterlife. The preserved fruit mixed in with a dense cake was thought to withstand the journey. That's why I take it winter camping. It lasts forever, and contains an insane amount of nutrients.

2 ¾ cups flour
1 tsp Baking Powder
½ lb butter
1 cup white sugar
3 eggs
¼ tsp salt
2 tsps vanilla
½ lb sugared cherries
1 lb bleached sultana raisins
½ cup warm water

Cut fruit up into small bits and add them to the mixture of the remaining ingredients. Place in a cooking pan with a removable bottom, lined with parchment paper. Bake at 300 degrees for 2 to 3 hours. The longer it ages the better it tastes.

Basic Bannock

This is a staple for me during long trips in every season. It's a recipe that all campers should have memorized, and then experiment with other add on ingredients (i.e. cinnamon bannock for breakfast or Cajun-spice bannock for lunch).

½ cup white flour
½ cup whole wheat flour
1 tsp baking powder
3 tbsp. powdered milk
½ tsp salt

Mix all dry ingredients, and add water slowly until dough is slightly sticky. Separate into 3-4 patties and fry in an oiled frying pan over moderate heat until both sides are a golden brown.

Logan Bread

One of my all-time favorite desserts to create out there in the woods is Logan bread. It contains everything needed on a cold trip: calories, nutrition, long shelf-life and great taste.

Logan bread gets its name from an expedition team who set out to summit Mount Logan, Alaska, in 1950. Rather than the usual hard tack the climbers created a kind of do-it-yourself energy-bar. Like any recipe, however, there's some debate over the original ingredients used in the founding recipe. However, the common components have stayed the same. It's the added bonuses, like raisins or chocolate chips, that have been altered.

1 ½ cups whole wheat flour
1 ½ cups unbleached all-purpose flour
    (rye-flour is thought to be what was
    originally used)
1 ¼ cups rolled oats
¾ cup lightly packed brown sugar
1½ tsp baking powder
1 tsp salt
2 eggs
1 cup applesauce
½ cup liquid honey
½ cup canola oil
¼ cup molasses
1 cup raisins
⅔ cup sunflower seeds

Most prepare this at home, taking advantage of using the fresh ingredients (eggs) and avoiding the hassle of carrying separate containers of liquid ingredients (honey, molasses, apple sauce). It's a wise choice, and the bread has a long shelf-life. But it's possible to make it fresh in while in the interior. Here's how:

In a large pot, combine flours, rolled oats, sugar, baking powder and salt. In a second pot, stir together eggs (powdered eggs will do or substitute with 1/2 cup of powdered milk), applesauce, honey, oil and molasses. Pour liquid ingredients into dry ingredients. Stir just until well blended. Stir in raisins and sunflower seeds. Divide batter into two greased 9 inch (23 cm) square pans. Bake in a reflector oven, against hot coals, or use a Dutch oven or any other deep-dish baking pan. Bake for 45 minutes or until the top of the bread springs back when lightly pressed. Remove and allow to cool for 10 minutes before cutting into squares or bars.

DARE TO BE DIFFERENT
Rather then add raisins or sunflower seeds, add cranberries, almonds, walnuts or chocolate chips. Try substituting canola oil with coconut oil.

Hard Tack

This stuff lasts forever, in all types of temperature extremes. That's why it was taken on long sea voyages (and winter treks) and given other names like pilot bread, cabin bread, ship biscuit, sea biscuit or sea bread. Soldiers in the American Civil War also called it tooth dullers, molar breakers, or sheet iron. It doesn't sound very appetizing but dipping it in a warm cup of tea or crumbling it into a soup on a cold winter day along the trail is divine.

3 cups white flour
2 tsp salt
1 cup water

Mix the flour, water and salt together, making sure the contents stay fairly dry. Roll it out, keeping it at about 1/2-inch thick, and cut it into rectangles 3 inches x 3 inches. Poke holes on the top with a common nail. Place on a non-greased cooking sheet and bake at 350 degrees for half-an-hour. Let it stand and harden for a few days and, when it has the consistency of a brick, it is ready to pack on your trip.

Bacon and Potato Soup

Soup is a winter campers long lost love. It's soothing, comforting, nutritious and tastes amazing.

6 thick slices American bacon
1 ½ tps olive oil
½ cup chopped onion
½ cup chopped carrots
1 stalk celery (chopped)
1 chicken bouillon cup
4 potatoes
⅛ tsp cayenne pepper
½ cup shredded Cheddar cheese
½ tsp kosher salt

Fry bacon until crisp. Place aside. In another frying pan (or at least wipe out the excess bacon grease), pour olive oil. Add cut up onion, carrot and celery for about 3-4 minutes. Mix in chicken bouillon cube, potatoes, and pepper. Bring to a boil and then simmer. It's done when the potatoes are soft. Add the cheese and let it melt. Break bacon into bits and sprinkle on top.

HISTORY OF THE S'MORE

At times making dessert may seem too time consuming. It's not. Don't fall into the routine of handing out chocolate bars to everyone to munch on around the campfire. That's not dessert. Besides, desserts can be quite simple to make. Caramel pudding served with a shot of Grand Marnier is better than a stale cookie. Just look at the history of the S'more. Since its creation, camping has definitely stepped up a notch.

S'mores have been a camp tradition ever since the recipe first appeared in the 1927 edition of the Girl Scout handbook "Tramping and Trailing." And there's no doubt why it was given its name – short for "some more." Think about it. Kids get to pierce a sugary marshmallow with a stick, hold it over the campfire until it ignites, then squish it between two chunks of chocolate and two Graham crackers (some campers have been known to toss the crackers).

Similar to most recipes the s'more wasn't completely original. Products with a comparable recipe (marshmallows, chocolate and graham crackers) entered the market place prior to the Girl Scout manual. Moon Pies were introduced in 1917 and Mallomars were on the store shelves as early as 1913.

Marshmallows, the key ingredient to a s'more, have an even longer history. Egyptians would squeeze the sweet sap from the mallow plant growing in wild marshes and add honey for flavor. By the mid-1800s the treat had reached France when owners of a small candy store whipped, sweetened and molded the gummy sap.

It didn't take long for the natural mallow to be replaced by gelatin and modified cornstarch. In 1948 a marshmallow manufacture, Alex Doumark, had the idea of pushing the sticky substance through a long pipe and cut it to the shape we're used to seeing. A couple years later some other manufacture had the idea of injecting air, giving the marshmallow its fluffy, light texture.

To date no one seems to know who actually started the act of toasting a marshmallow over a campfire and transforming the white spongy puff into a burned carbon shell with a sticky, tongue-burning centre. It was probably some camp counselor that couldn't stand baking up another can of pork and beans. But it's in the United Stated where most are now consumed — 90 million pounds per year to be exact. The majority of those consumers are no surprise under the age of twelve. It seems the older one gets the less inviting toasting a marshmallow becomes. Most adults, 56% in fact, prefer eating it raw. Truth is, parents secretly despise them; and they especially loathe the making of s'mores on camping trips. The problem is that the gooey mess will undoubtedly get all over the kid's cloths.

CHAPTER 8

Health and Safety

Cold injuries

WINTER CAMPING has GAINED a problematic stigma of being far more dangerous than summer camping. Both have safety concerns and avoidances, and both are less hazardous than driving the busy highway to and from your camping trip. However, winter does have one additional concern. Due to the cold temperatures, if something does go wrong it can turn deadly very quickly.

Sadly, it seems more people are getting injured out there than ever before. Deaths and evacuations have more than doubled. Of course, the big question is: why? It could be simple math. More people are heading out in the woods. It could also be that more high-tech gadgets are now available to call for help. I'm thinking these are meager points. The real truth behind the issue is that a good majority of campers just aren't skilled enough to be out there in the first place.

We live in a society where information is quickly and easily obtained. That's a good thing. But wilderness skills can't be learned quickly and easily. They take time. Yet we don't seem to have the patience — or even desire — to take the time. Watching YouTube videos on how to fix a toilet doesn't make you a trained plumber, and the same goes with lighting a fire or erecting a tarp. Practice makes perfect.

The worst part, however, is that fewer people will want to go out. It's easier

A thermometer makes a great camp gadget to bring along. On second thought, maybe it's a good idea not to know how cold it really is.

just to stay at home. Recently a school in Toronto, Ontario cancelled their annual winter camping trip. The program was over twenty years old. The new decision was based on two main reasons — the liability was too high (or perceived to be) and there was little interest from the students in going camping. The second point is the one I'm really worried about. The fewer people we have going out there, the less wilderness will be protected.

We have to reach the masses and talk sense with them — let them know what my mother, who has a strong Scottish disposition, always told me before heading out into the winter woods.

"Dinnea be stupid!"

That's what she would blurt out every time I'd head out on a trip, and she still gives me that sage advice. Seems harsh — but being logical about things while you're out there makes the most sense. Prevention is the key. If the ice doesn't look safe, then don't cross it. If a storm is approaching, then hunker down and wait for it to be over. Just... dinnea be stupid!

Hypothermia

It's true what they say, hypothermia kills. The "big chill" afflicts more people than any other outdoor calamity. It's more of a concern, however, during the shoulder seasons — spring and fall — when it's around freezing and very wet. In the winter, you're more acclimatized to the cold and, as long as you stay dry, you're safe from hypothermia. Remember what our mothers once taught us — dress for the weather.

The general rule is not to sweat. Slow yourself down. It may sound counterintuitive, but activities that heat you up and make you sweat lead to rapid heat loss. Your body sweats to cool itself down. At the same time it will dampen the body, and can chill you right into a state of hypothermia. Keep moving to stay warm, but don't overdo it.

SPOT TRACKING DEVICE

I personally wouldn't travel out in the woods without a tracking device, satellite phone or any other type of communication device. I may be old-fashioned when it comes to not bothering to send a tweet or text to share my deep feeling of what I'm experiencing while out in the woods, but I'd be a fool not to use a piece of technology that could save my life. My preference is the SPOT. I've used one for years. It tracks you, has an emergency distress button, and a button that sends a message and your location to friends and family at home.

All this advice doesn't mean anything if you fall through the ice. For this, it might be best to take some pointers from Dr. Gordon Giesbrecht, the world's leading authority on cold water immersion, rather than your mother.

Giesbrecht, director of the University of Manitoba's Laboratory for Exercise and Environmental Medicine, is the "King of the Big Chill" and takes his job very seriously. "Professor Popsicle" has, for the goodness of science, lowered his body temperature below 95 degrees (the inception of hypothermia) over three dozen times.

A key point Giesbrecht states is that the idea of immediately getting hypothermic the moment you take the plunge into cold water is false. The initial danger here is that instant gasp of breath one takes, which will end up drowning you if you submerge, inhale and panic. If you don't panic, control your breathing, and begin to slowly tread water or take hold of the ice edge around you, the "gasping" will subside within a minute or two. You will definitely go numb, but the pain of the cold will lessen and you'll have about ten minutes before your muscles react and the real cold sets in. You have that time to re-correct yourself or free yourself from the water. After that point your mind may not be rational, but your body has another hour before it reaches the critical point of being hypothermic.

So, what's cold? If you're cold-sensitive, then it's quite reasonable to feel the "shock" of the cold when the water temperatures are only 77°F (25°C), but on average it takes temperatures below 60°F (15°C) to become life-threatening.

The immersion time is obviously increased by what you're wearing. But remember, hypothermia can be deadly. Prevention is the key. Having enough smarts to not get into a dangerous predicament in the first place is what's going to keep you alive.

I once treated two people for hypothermia. It was later fall/early winter and a group of canoeists had decided to go paddling on a lake that hadn't completely frozen over yet. It was a foolish endeavor that almost led to their demise.

By the time some friends and myself removed them from the water, both were in a state of panic and showing the first signs of hypothermia — awkward motor control, minor mental confusion, uncontrollable shivering and, worst of all, a constant denial that they were in trouble. The victims were dangerously hypothermic. Their body temperature had dropped, shivering had stopped, one canoeist had lost consciousness and the other's mental status was severely limited, forcing him to become uncontrollably convulsive.

At this stage, we had only one choice of action. We immediately removed all their wet clothing, since this is what conducts heat away from the body almost 30 times quicker than usual, and placed them in sleeping bags. Then we crawled in the sleeping bags with them, and attempted to warm their bodies with our own body heat.

Thankfully the incident happened close to a major road and we had the luxury of calling for an ambulance. If it was on a remote trip, however, we would have had to continue warming their bodies up with hot (non-caffeinated and non-alcoholic) drinks, high-calorie snacks, a warm fire and a hot pack placed over the major blood vessels in the neck, armpit, and groin.

For extreme cases, the medical treatment would have been even more invasive. Cardiopulmonary resuscitation and cardiac massage must be given to a patient whose heart has stopped. This must be maintained until the patient is re-warmed and shows a pulse. In the hospital, people have survived after hours of resuscitation efforts.

Frostbite and frostnip

Frostbite can occur when temperatures reach below 32°F (0°C), and in most cases is the cause of extreme wind chill against exposed skin (nose, cheeks, ear lobes) or the lack of blood circulation in fingers and toes. It's similar to a burn where the skin tissue is damaged. A mild case, labeled frostnip, is more common and can be easily treated in the field by sharing body heat (skin-to-skin) with someone else. I've placed my fingers in my trip partner's armpit. Immersing the area is warm (not hot) water is also effective. Don't rub or massage the area. You will just damage the skin.

Frostnip is more recognizable then frostbite — the skin becomes white or

Moose-hide leather mitts are far better than gloves in keeping the fingers from becoming frostnipped.

waxy-looking — and it's important you keep watch for these early signs. Once you get frostbite, the treatment isn't that easy. The skin tissue is frozen and most likely dead by this point, and the victim needs professional medical care before permanent damage occurs. Severe blistering is common and even amputation of the damaged area can occur.

If immediate evacuation of the victim is impossible, then it's best not to attempt warming up the frozen area, only to have it exposed to the cold again and making things extremely worse. Just isolate the injury the best you can.

The best way to prevent both frostbite and frostnip is simply to cover up. The less exposed skin, the less change of injury. Wear a hat, hood or balaclava. Mitts are better than gloves to keep your fingers moving and warm.

Wind burn

The moment a cold wind hits exposed skin, it quickly begins robbing your body of heat. This is known as wind chill. It can also "burn" the skin. The more the wind increases, the more dramatically the wind chill decreases. For example: –22°F (–30°C) drops to –78°F (–61°C) with a wind speed of 25 mph (40 kph). At this point, skin will freeze in less than 30 seconds.

Drink lots of water. You'd think the opposite applies, but winter traveling conditions are similar to being in a dry desert environment.

Dehydration

A lot of winter campers suffer from dehydration without knowing it. A winter landscape is like a desert — dry and arid. The problem is, it doesn't appear that way. Put that together with the hassle of retrieving fresh water and you end up not drinking enough fluids. This is the number one reason campers get nauseous, have headaches, lose their appetite, become constipated or have constant diarrhea, and generally feel irritable. You need to drink at least 3 to 4 quarts (3-4 L) of water per day, replenishing it slowly throughout the day (about a quart an hour). Swallowing a huge amount in the morning makes it impossible for your body to process it all, and gulping it down at night doesn't help one little bit. The moment your mouth becomes dry or you crave a drink, it's too late.

Your body's fluids are too low. A cup of coffee or tea doesn't help, either. Caffeine is a diuretic and will actually increase the loss of body fluids. Alcohol will do the same. A well-hydrated camper pees frequently and has clear urine. Deep yellow urine, with a strong odor, is a true sign of not drinking enough fluids.

Snow-blindness

I've had snow blindness and it hurts. It feels like campfire coals placed directly on your eyeballs. It happened when I spent the full day hauling my load across a large frozen lake, in bitter cold but in full sunshine. I protected my face from the wind but not my eyes from the sun. The pain didn't come until halfway through the night while I was snug in my sleeping bag. That's the worst time to deal with any

AVALANCHES

I've only witnessed one avalanche in my lifetime. It was during a backpacking trip in Jasper. Thankfully, I was at a safe distance. I heard a loud boom and then saw the massive snow load slide down the eastern slope of a far-off mountain. It took some rocks and trees along for the ride as well, leaving a path of destruction. I realized then how fast and unsuspecting avalanches can be to a traveler.

The best way to stay safe from avalanches is to avoid places where one could occur.

There are two types: loose snow avalanche and slab avalanche. The first begins at a single origin and then spreads out, collecting more snow as it goes. It usually happens after a heavy snowfall. The second is a big slab of snow that fractures off a slope and starts to tumble down the slope. The break is triggered by noise, or you traveling over it.

The best way to deal with avalanches is to be absolutely diligent while traveling where one could occur. Travel in wooded areas or ridgetops if you can, and stay away from gullies or the foot of steep pitches. When traveling in groups, spread yourself out, keep an eye on everyone, don't go ahead of anyone and don't have more than one person enter a problem area at a time. Keep an eye out for mini-avalanches or "snow sloughs." A bigger one in the same area is more than possible. Stay clear of new snow fallen on sun-crested snow. It's a hot spot for avalanches. And, just like traveling across a frozen lake, test the snow with a ski pole or long stick. Feel for consistency when plunging the pole in. If the resistance is uneven, with punches through now and then, stay clear and choose another route.

If you're caught in an avalanche, the best bit of advice is not to panic. Attempt to keep to the surface and get out of the main path of the slide. Make a swimming motion to counteract the rolling snow pulling you under. If you are completely covered, hold both of your arms in front of your face and push against the snow to provide an airspace prior to the snow hardening. Wait to be rescued. Statistics show that if you're located 10 minutes after the accident, you have an 85 percent chance of survival; an hour and you have a 55 percent chance.

Ski goggles go a long way in protecting yourself from snow blindness. Photo: Colin Angus

injuries. You're warm and toasty but you have to get up and fix yourself. Thankfully, I knew the problem when it happened.

My first remedy was to grab the old tea bag from my before-bedtime warm-up mug. Placing it over my eyes helped a bit but didn't fix the problem. I continued with cold compresses, which was actually a bit of snow cupped in my bandana I always wear around my neck. It worked better, but the pain persisted enough that I had to take a day off traveling and just lie in the tent with gauze wrapped around my eyes, waiting it out in total darkness.

Snow blindness is sunburn of the eyes. It happens when you don't protect your eyes from the harsh reflection of the sun against snow.

Prevention is easier than trying to heal the affliction. Trust me. Sunglasses, or better yet a pair of ski goggles, will do. For the fun of it, you can create a makeshift pair out of a piece of birch bark with slits cut lengthwise to see through, or look like a football player and rub charcoal from the morning fire under your eyes. It will help reflect the light.

Types of bleeding

Gentle ooze: This is like when you nick yourself shaving and the blood seeps slowly from the wound. It's known as capillary bleeding and will usually stop on its own or when you place a band-aid on it. The only thing you should be concerned about is the risk of infection.

Slow but steady stream: A sharp camp saw will do the trick for this one. The blood comes from a number of blood vessels, building up below the skin and then exiting the wound at a steady and sometimes alarming rate. Direct pressure at the exact source of the bleeding will work. It's usually not as bad as it looks. Take note that cuts to the head or face will usually produce a lot more blood. Use a sterile gauze pad and, if bleeding continues, place another gauze pad onto the blood-soaked one. Peeling off the first gauze will interrupt the clotting process.

Spurting and squirting: This isn't good. If the blood is streaming and pulsating out of the wound, then expect that an artery has been severed. Bleeding will be severe at several pints per minute. It must be stopped immediately. Place direct pressure on it even before getting proper dressing out of the first-aid kit. It will eventually clot, as long as the area is not moved about too much. In major cases a tourniquet must be used, but this is extremely rare; if done to a leg or arm, you must assume that amputation of the area later on is pretty much a given.

Burns

You have a higher chance to burn yourself winter camping than you do summer. Roaring campfires, hot cooking pots, scalding wood stoves in hot tents...

The good news is that you have a cooling agent nearby — snow. Usually you have to rinse the burn area with cool water. It's easier to use snow. Gently, of course. Use a cloth or your bandana.

Check the degree of the burn. If it's deep, you have to cover it with gauze and get out. But if it's just a surface burn, you can treat it on-site. Sanitize and cover the wound to stop infection. Infection runs rampant out on a trip. Continue to wash it, cool it, and cover it. Don't apply anything like butter or lard — that just traps the wound from breathing. To air is to heal.

Blisters

Remember, it's your feet that mainly get you around out there. So you can imagine how easily an outing can quickly turn disastrous when something as simple as a blister can make you disabled.

To avoid blisters forming on your feet, make sure your footwear is well broken in before your trip. If you happen to have a blister starting to form while on a trip, make sure to place a piece of moleskin on it right away. It

Making a fire is an essential skill in the winter.

can literally save the trip. Moleskin is a felt-like material that comes with a very adherent backing and is supplied in sheets that can be cut to the exact size and shape of the blister. Just make sure to clean and dry the skin before you apply it.

Another helpful product to toss in your first-aid kit is Second Skin. It's available in strips and is conveniently packed in a re-sealable foil envelope. After cutting off a strip, the plastic peels off one side and the gel film is placed on the skin. It can be held in place by a larger piece of moleskin.

Clean, well-fitting socks are also essential on any trip if you want to keep your feet free of blisters, not to mention to rid your tent of foot odor (which always seems to linger even after your tent partner has tossed your boots out the front flap of the tent). This pattern of changing your socks daily will also keep you safe from getting "trench foot." The aliment, which got its name from soldiers constantly standing in wet trenches during World War 1, is similar to frostbite in theory. Prolonged exposure to moisture and/or cold will create nerve and muscle damage. The results vary from just having a slightly swollen, discolored and tender foot to excessive swelling and blisters, which later form ulcers, leading to gangrene.

Personalize your first-aid kit

First-aid kits are one of those necessary evils. Rarely do you ever take it out of your pack to use it (at least, I hope that's the case). But the moment you need it, the kit quickly becomes one of the most important items to have brought along. What's even more crucial is that it contains the proper items to do the job.

I've always packed my own personal first-aid kit. I also sign up for a wilderness first-aid course at least every two years. That way I know exactly what's in the kit and have a good idea of how to use what's inside.

FIRST-AID KIT

- ☐ Band-aids (various shapes and sizes)
- ☐ Ace bandages (for sprained ankles or swollen knees)
- ☐ Butterfly bandages
- ☐ Gauze pads (various sizes)
- ☐ Feminine napkins (for soaking up blood from cuts and scrapes)
- ☐ Moleskin (for blisters)
- ☐ Iodine
- ☐ Alcohol swabs
- ☐ Sterile suture kit
- ☐ Safety pins
- ☐ Scissors (small)
- ☐ Eye patch
- ☐ Antiseptic cream
- ☐ Sunscreen
- ☐ Hand lotion (your dry hands will thank me)
- ☐ Lip balm
- ☐ Water purification tablets
- ☐ Throat lozenges
- ☐ Antacid tablets
- ☐ Laxative
- ☐ Extra-strength Tylenol or its equivalent
- ☐ Small pack of ibuprofen (for stopping inflammation)
- ☐ Tweezers
- ☐ Small mirror (for inspecting eye injuries... or giving yourself a clean shave)
- ☐ Adhesive tape
- ☐ Safety-pins
- ☐ First-aid manual (explaining everything from splints and treatment of shock to CPR)

Other items:

_____

_____

_____

_____

_____

Outside of fire, nothing may contribute to your comfort and leisure more than a well-chosen ax.

— Mors Kochanski

CHAPTER 9

Tools of the Trade

Ax debate

THE DAY ONE OF THE YOUNG MALE CAMPERS in our group wacked his groin with a hatchet was the day I decided never to bring an ax on a summer canoe trip again. It seemed to me, after flipping through my old journal entries, that the majority of really nasty injuries were connected to poor ax (or especially hatchet) handling. It therefore seemed logical to never pack one and depend on a camp saw. But I've had endless traditional campers say that leaving the ax at home is not the answer; showing the campers the right way to wield an ax in the woods is the best way to prevent an injury. They have a point. It may be possible to go summer camping without using an ax, but there is no way I'd ever go winter camping without one.

To safely split wood with a camp ax, I begin by sawing sections of a log. Anything smaller in diameter then my forearm I simply throw in the fire, but any piece bigger is split with the ax. I set the piece of wood upright, place the blade of the ax across the center of the log, and then strike the top of the ax head with another piece of wood. The ax works as an effective slitting edge rather than a cutting tool. No swinging is involved, which greatly decreases the chance of injury! And remember, a sharp ax is much safer than a dull one.

Here's how Paul Kirtley sharpens his ax: general-purpose axes have convex bevels. Even the wide, heavy heads of splitting axes are convex

Chop your own wood, and it will warm you twice.

close to the edge. The benefit of a convex bevel profile is a greater cross-section of metal close to the edge than a flat bevel, resulting in it being more robust and less likely to chip. That's why it's important to keep this bevel shape while also keeping your ax sharp.

To maintain the bevel profile of your ax, you need to sharpen it in such a way as to not only remove metal at the edge but evenly across the whole bevel. Sharpening stones and metal files are the tools of ax sharpening. Both tend to be flat. This means if you

place the stone or file at any point on a convex bevel, it will only be touching the bevel tangentially at this point.

So, to remove metal from the whole bevel, you need to vary the angle of the stone or file relative to the bevel. For this, it's better to use a short, compact stone, which can complete the full range of angles required to abrade the bevel, without being restricted by contact with other areas of the ax head.

Even with hatchets and small axes, it is easier to hold the ax still and move the stone relative to the ax. While you can use pocket slip stones to sharpen an ax, you do need to be very careful not to remove your fingertips.

A thicker stone allows you to hold the stone with your fingers and your fingers not to extend beyond the surface which is working the bevel. This means there is no chance of removing your fingertips.

If I need to remove more serious chips from the edge of an ax I also carry a metal file. I work the ax with the file first, then move onto the stone once I have sufficiently reshaped the bit. In fact, you can get an ax remarkably sharp with just a file.

As well as a convex bevel, most general-purpose axes have a curved bit, so you have curvature in two different planes. The upshot of this is that a circular-to-oval motion, with pressure being applied as the stone is moved towards the edge, is an efficient and fluid sharpening stroke.

Start with the stone's coarse side, work along the edge, then work back from the edge across the bevel again, then back the other way at a shallower angle still. Repeat until metal has been removed from the whole bevel. Do this again a few times. Then swap to the opposite bevel, making the same number of passes. Keeping the work you do on both sides broadly symmetrical is important to avoid losing symmetry in the bevel profile.

Ax sharpening is an art form. A thicker stone is a safer way to keep your fingertips. Photos: Paul Kirtley

Continue with the above methodology until the ax starts to feel sharp. Then switch to the fine side of your stone and repeat the whole process.

Camp saw

Before you split wood with an ax, you first need to saw it into sections. It's called bucking up firewood and it's a regular camp chore.

A camp saw is essential for winter camping. Problem is, there's more to know about the design of a saw than meets the eye. A good portable, aluminum-framed folding saw measures 24 inches. That means it can cut through a 6-inch diameter log without any hassles.

Saw blades come in different toothing patterns. One style comes with two types of teeth: cutting teeth and raking teeth. How it works is that the cutting teeth "cut" into the wood and the rakers scoop out the sawdust and bits of wood that were cut with the cutting teeth. Usually there's a three-to-one ratio for cutting teeth to raking teeth. It's a great tooth pattern for either dry softwoods (conifers like balsam and spruce) or green hardwoods (deciduous like maple or birch). It's the most versatile blade and comes with most saws. It's also the same one used in the old logging days to cut down the massive pine trees.

Next is the peg toothing pattern. It has only one type of tooth, which does both the cutting and the raking. It's best for dry hardwoods. The wood fiber of hardwood is tighter and denser and the sawdust created is a lot finer. This pattern is best to cut through faster. Dry hardwood is also the big bonus to find while winter camping. Soft wood is great to get the fire going, and a peg blade can still cut through it, but hard wood burns longer and hotter. This makes the peg tooth pattern the best overall winter camping blade.

Winter knife

There are two general knife designs: fixed or folding. Fixed knives are the traditional style with non-sliding and non-folding blades and made from a single piece of heat-treated, forged steel. It creates a strong and stable knife. A folding knife has the blade fold in and stored in the handle. High-grade folding knives are nice and compact, and the ones that lock when folded back out are safe to use. They're not my favorite in the winter, however, simply because they're difficult to unfold with cold hands wrapped in big mitts.

Camping knives come in two steel types, carbon steel and stainless steel. Carbon steel blades are known for their hardness and are easier to

Make sure to let the saw teeth do most of the work, and use the full length of the saw.

SAWING BASICS

- Start slow and set the teeth into the wood.
- Apply light pressure.
- Make sure not to twist the blade while pushing and pulling.
- Keep it perpendicular.
- Use the full length of the saw on each stroke.
- To keep a straight cut, make note of where you want the saw to go rather than where it is.
- Replace bent or dull blades (it's not worth trying to sharpen modern-day camp saw blades).

sharpen. Stainless steel is less prone to rust, takes far less maintenance and tends to hold its edge longer.

Knifes come with either full tangs or stick or "rat tail" tangs. The tang is the bit of steel that extends past the blade into the handle. Full tangs mean that the knife's blade is constructed from a single and continuous piece of metal, which gives the knife greater strength and rigidity. Campers who like splitting wood or "batonning" with their knife will use a full tang knife. Stick tang knifes have a reduced piece of metal extending into a cavity in the handle. They're not as robust, but are lighter and more agile. The only knife I bring is a smaller 69-mm laminated stainless steel blade, and I wear it around my neck rather than attached to my belt. The sheath around your neck makes it easy to get at without having to dig through layers of clothing to reach your belt.

Here's how Paul Kirtley sharpens his knife: consistent sharpening doesn't require expensive or complicated equipment. All you need on the trail is a compact sharpening stone and a leather belt.

There are many knife designs and various types of bevel. Single flat bevels, secondary bevels and convex bevels are common types. With any of them, the aim of sharpening is two-fold: one, to remove metal from each

Single flat bevels, secondary bevels and convex bevels are the most common types of knife designs. Photo: Paul Kirtley

bevel so the bevels meet at a fine cutting edge; two, to maintain the original shape of the bevels.

To start, place your knife flat on the stone and then tilt the knife towards the cutting edge until there is no gap between the cutting edge and the stone. If the knife has a flat bevel, then this is the constant angle at which you will sharpen. If the bevel is convex, you will have to vary the angle of the stone relative to the knife in order to remove metal from the entire bevel.

Start at the end of the stone nearest to you. With the cutting edge facing away from you, tilt the knife until you achieve the correct bevel angle. Move the knife away from you along the stone, applying pressure towards the leading edge of the knife.

Move the knife across the stone as

Two tools of the trade: Campfire saw and ax.

well as forwards so that you cover the entire length of the knife. Near to the end of the sharpening stroke, lift the handle slightly to maintain contact between any curved section of blade and stone.

Where metal has been removed from the bevel, it will show as obvious scratches or shiny areas. Use this to assess your technique, adjusting if necessary. To sharpen the opposite bevel, turn the cutting edge to face you on the far end of the sharpening stone, tilt the edge to the correct angle, then draw the knife along the stone towards you. To ensure you are removing metal equally from both bevels, you can count the number of sharpening strokes on each side of the knife, batching them in, say, groups of six.

The process creates a very thin foil of metal where the bevels meet. This foil or burr should be minimized to ensure a robust edge. Once you start to feel a distinct burr along the whole edge, switch to alternating sharpening strokes — left, right, left, right... Make at least 30 strokes.

Finally, to smooth the edge and remove any remaining burr, finish the process by stropping your knife on a leather belt. Run the blade along the unfinished leather inside the belt, leading with the back of the knife (i.e., with the sharp edge trailing). Alternate the stropping strokes back and forth 50 to 100 times.

To check to see if your knife is sharp, carefully run your thumb across the edge with no pressure. A sharp edge will catch the ridges of your thumbprint. A dull edge will not.

To check visually, orient yourself towards a light source and angle the knife to see any reflections from flat spots, which indicate a dull edge.

CHAPTER 10

Winter Travel

A MAJORITY OF WINTER CAMPERS simply throw everything into a backpack and head off into the winter woods on snowshoes or skis, following a marked trail or just bushwacking. It's an effective, lightweight approach to get around out there. I use the same backpack used for my summer and fall trips: an internal-frame pack, which places the weight snug against your back. With the load hugging your body, it's much easier to scramble up a hillside or cross-country ski across a frozen lake without losing your balance. Some winter trekkers prefer an external-frame backpack consisting of a lightweight aluminum or aluminum-alloy frame outside the main body which holds your equipment. As the frame is external, the weight of your gear is held away from your body and is evenly distributed between your shoulders and hips. With the load being held up on a frame, however, the pack will tend to sway back and forth while you walk along the trail, lessening your freedom of movement.

In the store, make sure to properly size the pack to your weight and build. If you purchase a cheaper, one-size-fits-all pack, make sure the adjustment straps have little give. A hip belt should conform to your hips, not your hips to the hip belt. Padded shoulder straps should have extra padding that provides comfortable cushioning and shape retention. Before you hike out with your new purchase, make sure to ask the salesperson to load the pack up with weight and walk around the store, just to make sure it fits nice and snug. Out on the trail is no place to discover you've made the wrong choice.

The lighter the load, the more wilderness landscape you get to experience.

Lightening your load

It seems the older I get, the wiser I become about packing light for a backpacking trip. On my last trip, I stripped down my gear considerably and still was able to have a good time out there.

The first rule I have is to set out my "must-have" items and figure a way to reduce the weight of them. Second, I look at how to use items of camp gear for multiple functions. And third, I re-think my luxury items and make a firm decision whether they're worth the weight.

Here are a few more tips (and some gear choices) that have really helped lighten my load:

Stuff sacks: Compression sacks are a must if you want to reduce bulk in your pack. Bulk is sometimes more noteworthy then weight. One of the best systems is the air-purge — sacks that are waterproof, with excess air squeezed out while compressing. They're great for storing sleeping bags, clothes or a tent. You can't go wrong with purchasing a few different sizes.

Aquatabs. They're good for viruses, bacteria and Giardia cysts. You have to wait 30 minutes before the water is safe to drink, but the weight savings is incredible.

Cooking utensils: Switch to a Lexan spork and titanium pots. They can be expensive, but the weight reduction is worth the cost.

Clothes: Don't overdo it with clothes. You just need an extra layering system from what you are wearing and one shirt, pants, a few extra pairs of socks, and extra underwear. Merino wool is amazing. It's lightweight, reduces body odor and is really cozy to wear.

Down sleeping bag: Down is generally lighter and easier to compress than any other insulating material. I also find it warmer.

Tent: The smaller the tent, the warmer you'll be. Pack the body and the fly in separate compression sacks. It fits better in your pack that way.

A little bit of everything: Be religious about measuring out proper portions of things like toilet paper, paperback novels, snacks and anything else you wouldn't necessarily need a full container of for the amount of time spent out there.

Makeshift pillow: There is no real need to pack a pillow when you can simply use your clothes bag as a substitute.

Lithium batteries: By using lithium batteries instead of alkaline, you're cutting the weight by 50 percent. They also last three times longer and they are much better in cold temperatures.

Water tablets: Eliminate your water filter altogether and replace it with water tablets. It cuts your weight down considerably. I've been packing MSR

Winter campers have a huge advantage. You've got a slippery surface over which to pull your gear rather than having to strap it to your back.

Pulling your weight — sleds, pulks and toboggans

Winter campers have a huge advantage. You've got a slippery surface to pull your gear across rather than strapping it to your back. You might as well bring a few extra luxuries with you and haul it on a sled, pulk or toboggan.

If you're just starting out, the simplest design is the best. My first winter camping trip where I hauled my gear rather than carried it, I borrowed my daughter's plastic pull sled

purchased at the hardware store.

The next season I progressed to constructing my own pulk — basically, a wider sled with higher sides. I could have bought a professional expedition pulk, but I made a knock-off instead. My base was a durable plastic cargo sled that ice anglers use to pull behind their snowmobiles. I bought the smallest, and the cheapest.

The name "pulk" comes from the

Where should you place the pulling harness for hauling a toboggan? It's a huge debate in the winter trekking world. Some choose over the shoulder, others across the chest or around the waist.

Norwegian "pulkha", which is what natives of Lapland called their small sledges hauled by people or reindeer. It's been around for a long time. It's also easy to make one on your own.

The first step is to drill ¼-inch holes at even intervals (8 to 10 inches/20–25 cm apart) along the outside edge of the plastic sled. A thin rope or parachute cord is then laced crisscross through the holes to be used to lash your gear

in. Another technique is to lace the rope through the holes, but to tie loops at each section between the drilled holes. Bungee straps can then be used to attach to the loops and pulled over the gear to hold it down. Drill another hole in the back end of the sled and tie in a piece of 6-foot (1.8 m) cordage. This is used to help with holding the weight of the sled back while going down steep hills.

The hauling system can be made of medium cordage or PVC pipe. I prefer PVC pipe. It gives you better steering control and, more importantly, stops the sled from smashing into you on downhill sections. Any rigid material will work, but PVC pipe is the cheapest and easiest to work with.

I attached the pipe to the sled by either pushing the length of rope through the hollow pipe or drilling holes through one end, looping the cordage through it, doing the same to the front of the sled, and then attaching both loops with a metal clasp or carabiners. The two pipes were attached in the same manner to an old backpack belt harness I had. The important part is that I crisscrossed the PVC pipe. This helps when hauling around tight corners. If the pipe is straight, the sled will flip over. Having the pipe crisscrossed eliminates that.

Toboggans are the most flexible for hauling. Traditionally they have

WINTER WANNIGAN

"My interest in the wannigan began as a young canoe tripper at the Taylor Statten Camps and developed to a serious love affair as I progressed as a backcountry guide. My husband Mike shares my passion and is also a talented woodworker. For my birthday a few years ago, he presented me with a gorgeous custom-made wannigan. It fits my reflector oven perfectly and has a removable cutlery tray. With a leather tump and a capacity to hold our kitchen gear and about two weeks' worth of food, it now has a special place on all of our trips and in my heart.

The Wannigan, adapted for winter use, makes a great storage container when attached to the toboggan.

For a few winter trips we used a regular summer wannigan, but as we are always interested in improving our gear and systems we were in need of a wannigan that was custom-designed for winter and our sleds. The wannigan Mike built is lower in height than a typical summer wannigan, as well as a few inches longer, so you still have an excellent amount of space. It was built to fit on our sleds and the lower height makes it a more stable load. In lieu of a tump strap — as we don't intend to carry this one — we made two webbing straps with buckles to secure the lid. The handles are a little bit wider to give you a better grip when wearing mitts. Once in the tent, the lid can be removed and put across the top along with the removable cutlery tray — this makes for a great table! The cutlery tray slides easily across the inside for easy access to all areas. There is also an interior compartment to hold our kerosene lantern. It has a layer of epoxy along the walls to keep any leaks contained. We travel with the lantern empty and the fuel in a separate container."

— *Mercede Rogers*

Duffel bags offer a good solution to storing gear on your toboggan.

been made of hardwood (birch wood) planks, 10 feet (3 m) long, tapered with four to five wooden crossbars. The flexibility would keep the toboggan in full contact with the snow, perfect for hauling across flat frozen lakes or trails with a moderate slope. Going up and down anything more extreme in elevation would be a problem, however.

Wooden toboggans can still be purchased, but most winter campers purchase one made with an ultra-high molecular weight polyethylene (UHMWPE); basically, a high-density slippery plastic material. The cross-bars are made of hardwood (ash), attached by stainless steel screws. They come in various lengths. I own a 10-foot (3 m) and an 8-foot (2.5 m). The width is 15 inches (38 cm). Keep in mind that the narrower the tobog-gan, the easier it pulls. The wider it is, however, the less it will tip over. Being 15 inches (38 cm) seems to fit well inside the snowshoe trail you create in front of it.

To haul the toboggan, pull lines are connected at the front. They're attached relatively low to keep the nose up out of the soft snow. A good harness is made of rope and a wide strip of nylon seat-belt material. The pull line is also made adjustable, to be switched up in various terrain. Where you place the harness is a huge debate in the winter trekking world. Some choose over the shoulder, others across the chest or around the waist. Some even place it across the forehead or behind the neck, over the shoulders and under the arms. The answer is whichever seems most comfortable to you. I tend to change it up a bit now and then, just to break the boredom and move the pain in the body somewhere else for a while. You also need a 6-foot (1.8 m) length of rope attached to the back to help lower the toboggan downhill.

A toboggan can become exceedingly difficult to pull after a fresh snowfall or when the bottom of the sled frosts up overnight. Make sure to bring a scraper (I use an old credit card) to remove the frost and apply ski wax. To test it out, throw loose snow on the bottom of the toboggan. Re-scrape and apply more wax where clumps of snow stick.

Packing your gear

Whether you are using a sled, pulk or freight toboggan, the key to packing everything is to keep the load as low as possible and weight up front. You don't want everything tipping over on tight corners or when pulling over logs or big, fluffy snow drifts. If you're a canoeist, think of it as properly trimming your canoe.

Duffel bags make the best storage systems. Rubbermaid containers also work well, especially for storing kitchen gear and food. It's a cheap version of a winter wannigan. Just use bungee cords or rope to lash everything down. Don't go too cheap with the duffle bags, though. Poor-quality zippers will freeze and refuse to open (Vaseline or lip balm will help) and you'll need to keep the things stored inside waterproof somehow. If I'm hot tenting, I store my gear and tent in duffels and lash my stove onto the back — it's the lightest. I also attach one small duffel or day pack where I store day-use gear (i.e., water, snacks, extra gloves, extra layers...). You can even wrap the entire contents with your ground tarp to keep things contained, neat and tidy. It's a cheap version of what traditional winter trekkers call a "tank," a piece of canvas that's tied on the toboggan permanently and wraps around all the gear to keep things organized. Tierney Angus suggests that milk crates are great for food storage on the toboggans. You can fit the contents of one summer canoe barrel into two milk crates, which can then be turned into chairs or tables.

Snowshoes

When dealing with traditional wooden snowshoes, there are more designs than you'd think. For walking across flat, semi-open terrain, the proper style would be the Michigan or Algonquin snowshoe. It's the most common model and is shaped like a teardrop with its tail lagging behind to track a straight line and keep the tip out of the snow.

In hilly or mountainous country, the standard bear-paw style is more commonly used. With no tail, it makes walking easier. I also use the bear-paw in early spring for walking through deep, crusty, corn snow.

The other main styles of snowshoe

THE ART OF SNOWSHOEING

- Walking with snowshoes lashed to your feet is little different than strolling down the sidewalk wearing a pair of sneakers, except the width of the snowshoe forces you to swing each foot around in a semi-circular motion.
- Ski poles help to keep your balance and assist you to get up when you actually do fall down.
- Lurch forward on every step and let the snowshoe sink into the snow a bit to get a firm grip for the follow through step.
- To turn, kick straight out (with the left leg if you're going left and vice-versa if you're going right). Then twist 180 degrees with that leg and follow through with the other leg (ski poles will help you greatly here).
- Descend a hill in a zigzag pattern and lean back a little. Make sure the bindings are tight enough to keep your toes in place. And if the slope is too steep, place one foot in front of the other, sit on the back snowshoe, and slide down.
- Make sure to also zigzag uphill and make good use of your ski poles.
- Be happy you're bow-legged. It's definitely a plus.

New-age snowshoes vs. the traditional kind. It all depends on the snow conditions.

are the Ojibwa and the Alaskan. The Ojibwa is used for open areas, with its long length and upturned toe giving extra support and stability. The shoe's tip is pointed, looking like the back end of the Michigan or Algonquin style, and can actually help cut through the hard crust of snow or push away small saplings when walking in dense bush. The Alaskan is quite similar, except the toe is rounded.

All these styles are made of wood and lacing. However, outdoor stores are now more apt to carry the new-age snowshoes made of lightweight plastic or anodized aluminum equipped with mini-crampon bindings. Personally, I still prefer the wooden type. The new-age ones, even though they are lightweight and generally effective in moderate snow depths, are not good

LAMPWICK BINDINGS

"There are a number of ways to secure your foot to wood-framed snowshoes, but nothing quite compares to the simple elegance of traditional lampwick bindings. Lampwick bindings are incredibly lightweight, inexpensive, secure and comfortable. Unlike rubber bindings, lampwick won't stretch if you're pulling hard uphill, and with no buckles or cord locks to deal with they can be donned and doffed easily even if they've gotten wet and frozen hard. Lampwick is light enough and cheap enough that you can have a spare pair on your body at all times to replace a broken binding. But best of all, traditional lampwick bindings can be slipped on and off completely hands-free! The convenience of twisting into the snowshoes to slip out to the water hole to fill the pots at night, or a quick jaunt to the forest edge to relieve

oneself, has to be experienced to be fully appreciated. In extreme circumstances this could also be a safety feature, allowing you to slip off your snowshoes if you ever find yourself plunged into fast-moving water.

Two 5-foot (1.5 m) lengths of 1-inch (2.5 cm) cotton lampwick are all that you need to tie lampwick bindings. Prior to the introduction of woven cotton by Europeans, tanned moosehide thong was historically used, and today cotton 'shaker tape' and nylon webbing are both used with good results. We continue to use simple cotton lampwick and have had little incentive to look elsewhere. Ends should be sealed by dipping in melted beeswax or paraffin to prevent fraying (or melted to seal in the case of nylon).

We first learned how to tie the lampwick binding from Garrett Conover and Alexandra Conover-Bennett's *Snow Walker's Companion*, an exceptional source for

Lampwick bindings are incredibly lightweight, inexpensive, secure and comfortable.
Photos: Dave Marrone

all things traditional winter camping.

The lampwick is attached to the snowshoe by the 'Indian Hitch.' What you want to eventually create are two loops: one vertical loop by the toe opening on the snowshoe and one horizontal loop that passes over your heel. Begin with a piece of lampwick: approximately 5-foot (1.5 m) lengths of 1-inch (2.5 cm) cotton lampwick. Place your foot on the snowshoe and locate the open spots on the weave of the snowshoe directly beside the left and right side of your foot. Now, pass the lampwick down through both spaces, and then bring the lampwick back up through the toe hole. Remove your foot and pull about half the lampwick through on one side and start wrapping it around itself. Keep wrapping until you reach the top/center of your foot. Do the same on the other side, but first place your foot back in and pull the lampwick snug around the top of your foot. Now remove your foot and begin wrapping. Once that's done, check how your toe fits in — it should be nice and secure. Then you pass the lampwick to the back of the foot and secure with a simple overhand knot, tying it tight around the heel.

To put your foot into the Indian Hitch binding, you first anchor the snowshoe with the other foot. Slide your toe into the back horizontal (back) loop, then continue with the heel. Keep your foot pointed outwards, to the side of the snowshoe. Then pivot, slide the heel back, raise the heel, and then poke your toe through the vertical (front) loop. Repeat for the other snowshoe, anchoring with the other snowshoed foot. Do the reverse to remove the binding."

— *Dave and Kielyn Marrone,*
Lure of the North

enough for deep snow. With that said, however, if you're not going on some major trek in the far north where snow depths are an issue, then a lightweight pair will definitely do.

Having the perfect binding to hold your foot in place is extremely critical. There's nothing worse than messing around with an awkward binding system when your hands are numb with cold. There's an endless assortment, ranging from the simple Native hitch to a piece of old inner tubing. The most common binding, however, is a combination of a wide toe-piece and a leather-heel strap with a cross-strap over the instep. A single ski pole also comes in handy when trying to keep your balance in deep snow or trudging up steep inclines.

Boots

After the binding comes the boot. Oil-tanned moccasin boots, worn with one light pair and one heavy pair of wool socks, work great. I prefer winter mukluks. Not in wet snow, however — my feet will soon become soaked. I find a good old pair of felt-lined boots with rubber bottoms and leather tops to be adequate. They're on the heavy side, give me blisters, and at times can be too warm to wear comfortably, but with an extra pair of interchangeable liners in my pack I haven't lost a toe from frostbite yet.

SNOWSHOE REPAIR IN THE BUSH

"A number of years ago, four of us were on a winter trip in Northern Ontario. One of the guys was gathering firewood in the bush and bridged his snowshoes between two fallen trees buried in the snow. Snap! It was a jagged hinge break, with the ash frame still holding together at the top surface. Facing several days of trekking with only one snowshoe was a dismal prospect for the entire group. Unsettling as it was, I had experienced a similar break on one of my snowshoes 25 years earlier, so I knew it was merely a setback. Although the snowshoes were relegated to being a spare, they were still in regular use.

That time I had fixed my snowshoes at home using only a drill and some copper wire, but Jim suggested that for this break we apply spruce resin, used for centuries by Ojibwa and Cree as glue in the construction of bows, arrows and canoes.

So, armed with knives and a tin cup, off we went into the woods on a treasure hunt.

Finding white spruce in the boreal forest is easy. It's a large coniferous evergreen with scaly bark and four-sided, sharp and stiff needles that have an unpleasant odor not unlike

Boris Swidersky is a skilled winter camper with a few tricks up his sleeve, including knowing how to repair his traditional snowshoes on the trail.

cat urine. For something that smells so foul, a refreshing tea can be brewed from the needles. Until the 1920s, spruce gum, tasting of the great outdoors and sugar-free, was sold in stores as chewing gum. No trace of cat smell. Then it was replaced by the modern chiclet-based, sugar packed product.

To locate resin, we searched out trees that had damaged bark where the pitch had bled out and solidified into a hard, brittle mass. It didn't take long to fill the cup.

Back at camp we broke up the lumps of resin into powdery granules with the back of an ax on a block of wood and removed the larger bits of bark and needles. The resin was then returned to the cup and set on the wood stove to melt.

It is best not to use your favorite mug for this, because you will never remove all traces of resin. Also try not to overheat the resin as the resulting product will be weaker. If the resin catches fire, blow it out and move your container to a cooler part of the stove.

Then we whittled some small wood pegs and, using an awl from the tool kit, drilled a series of holes into the snowshoe frame through both sides of the break. Once the resin was melted, we added one part powdered charcoal from a partly burned stove log. This was to help temper the resin and make it easier to work. We also added a quantity of bacon fat, otherwise the final glue would be as brittle as glass.

The mixture of resin, charcoal and fat was thoroughly stirred with a stick and very carefully and liberally applied to the break. Do not, repeat, do not get a drop of hot resin on your skin. It sticks and burns. The break was closed and pegs driven into the holes to hold the repair in place. The whole thing was then wrapped tightly with snare wire and the snowshoe set aside for the resin to cool and harden.

And that was it. The snowshoe was fit for hard use and had acquired some character into the bargain. The trip could continue. And it did."

— *Boris Swidersky*

Skis

Cross-country/ backcountry skis

Cross-country skis are a quick and enjoyable way to get around out there — as long as the landscape and conditions allow for it. They're not the same as one would use on a well-groomed trail. Backcountry skis are wider, shorter, heavier, more durable and have a metal edge.

The "camber" of the ski is basically the arc under your foot. This area creates the "kick" where the ski grabs the snow before you glide across it. If the camber sags on the snow, you won't glide very well. Skis for a groomed trail are double camber. They give you more trim and more glide. In deep snow, however, you want less camber: a camber or camber and a half. That will give you more flex and the ability to engage in the snow and still get a better grip. It's not fast, but more efficient. If you have too much camber, you'll end up slipping and not getting a good grip.

A backcountry ski also has a stiff "flex" on its tip and tail. This keeps the grip pocket raised up from the snow

Mark Williamson heads across Algonquin Provincial Park on skis for 23 days, rather than using snowshoes. An epic trip! Photo: Mark Williamson

AT ONE WITH THE WORLD

"I set out on skis to climb up to the plateau one winter's day. The weather was cold and clear but I knew it could change rapidly. The ascent over I stripped off my climbing skins and reveled in a fast ski over the smooth snow into the heart of the plateau. Soon I could no longer see beyond this white world. Nothing existed except the snow and the mountains."

— *Chris Townsend*

Chris Townsend stops for the night after ascending, with skis, one of the many mountain peaks in northern Scotland. Photo: Chris Townsend

during the glide, giving you speed but also a solid grip when you need it.

Wax on or wax off

The wax zone is the kick zone, the area that provides grip before you glide. It needs to hold you steady before gliding but also glide while you're trying to move forward. A waxless ski has ridges to connect to the snow rather than wax. It's less maintenance and hassle. Waxing skis can be a science experiment, especially when the weather and snow conditions change throughout the day. If you're hauling a sled, however, wax skis will reduce the times you slip backwards. Mind you, if temperatures are warm, hovering around 32°F (0°C), then trying to wax your skis properly can be incredible frustrating. I'd go for the waxless. You could also consider using "skins." They're strips of cloth with backwards-pointing hairs that allow your ski to glide

Campers remove an ice chunk from skis with some hot water. Photo: Dan Cooke

in one direction and provide grip in the other. Great for using in mountainous conditions.

Backcountry ski boots

I find the best backcountry ski boot is one that's full leather or leather/synthetic and goes past the ankle. I'd also highly recommend that you get boots half a size bigger so you can add another layer of wool socks. Ski boots are cold when you're not moving. Change into new socks and camp boots as soon as possible when you stop for the night.

SKI BINDINGS AND SLUSH

"What about those step-in style of bindings? They are not well suited for the possible encounters with slush. Often if you run into slush, you need to take off the ski to scrape the ski bottom, but the binding has slush in it as well and can freeze up and not allow the binding to grip the metal rod as the mechanism is frozen in place. So hot water can be run into the binding to get the slush melted out of it. That is why I still use 3-pin bindings, as you can always chip out any ice buildup."

— *Dan Cooke, Cooke Custom Sewing*

CHAPTER 11

Ice

Ice conditions

I SHOULD HAVE THOUGHT THINGS THROUGH FIRST before I called the police. I had just moved to a small town, near a lake. It was a late winter and the ice was slow to form, and when it did it wasn't very stiff. I put my auger through at just under 2 inches (5 cm). So when I saw some local ice anglers out, I contacted the authorities. I wasn't the only one concerned. A number of my neighbors, who had lived there for well over thirty years, were yelling at the idiots to get off the ice. They threw back a few curse words and let all the bystanders know that they knew what they were doing. They obviously didn't. Not only was the ice too thin, they were fishing at a spot where the neighbors knew an underground spring came bubbling up — one of the worst places to be.

The police arrived and agreed the fishermen were idiots to be on the ice so early after freeze-up. They also told us that they couldn't arrest anyone for being an idiot. The police had no authority to tell them to get off the ice.

Traveling on ice can be dangerous. It can also be a great way to get around out there in the winter. Spend just a few hours hauling through the thick bush in deep snow, and you'll realize why traveling across frozen water is a better option. It's an open landscape where wind-packed snow is commonplace.

Where ice can be extremely hazardous is when your knowledge of good ice conditions is limited. Gaining

Writer Hap Wilson takes extra precautions walking across unknown ice.

THE SOUND OF GOOD ICE

"Once you get accustomed to walking or skiing on ice, you can tell a lot about its structure by the sound it makes when striking it with a ski pole or walking stick. It's almost like checking the quality of firewood by tapping it with the back of an ax — a dull thud means the wood is punky, while a sharp retort means it's solid. Ice can be gauged the same way, in most instances, and true to tell whether the ice is good or not.

If ice is covered in snow, you have no idea if it's strong enough until you test it out; and to do this takes one step at a time and a plunge with the blade of the ax every few feet. An ax will deflect off the surface of the ice if it's thick enough to hold your weight; otherwise, if an ax penetrates the ice cleanly and water splurges up through the crack, it's time to back off and choose another route. One sure measure to check the security of ice, especially on rivers where there are often deadly currents, is to find fresh moose tracks where the ice has visibly allowed the half-ton animal to make the crossing safely. There are times when deer and moose have not made crossings successfully and have succumbed in the ice water, their carcasses showing up in the river in the spring, bloated and putrified."

— *Hap Wilson, writer and guide*

experience is fundamental — but gaining it also means heading out onto the ice. Beyond trekking with someone more knowledgeable than yourself, being overcautious is the next best thing.

The first point to go over is how ice begins to form. A body of water flips when winter begins to set in. The water on the bottom, which is coldest during the summer, rises to the surface, and the warm surface water sinks to the bottom. This sets everything in motion and the freezing begins.

Not all ice is the same. Clear ice — or what some call "blue ice" — is the densest. The liquid freezes without particles mixed in, like snow or slush. White ice is far less dense and forms when a flood of snow and slush refreezes. You'll probably notice air bubbles or larger air pockets throughout it. A grayish tone to the ice indicates water is present and is definitely not safe.

Safe ice guide

Note that all ice should be considered unsafe at first. River currents, snow depth, and the amount of times the ice has thawed and then re-frozen can be an important issue. Here are some good guidelines:

- 3 inches (7.5 cm) = extremely dangerous; don't even think about it.
- 4 inches (10 cm) = okay for figure skaters and ice anglers.
- 7 inches (18 cm) = just enough for snowmobiles.
- 8 to 12 inches (20-30 cm) = can handle a small car or all-terrain vehicle.

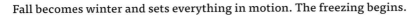

Fall becomes winter and sets everything in motion. The freezing begins.

The common rule out there is that you're safe walking on ice if it's 4 inches (10 cm). However, that statement is way too general. Each body of water is different, and should always be viewed that way. If it's white ice, then you can never trust a uniform thickness. If there are springs from groundwater or river mouths, then you're simply rolling the dice every step you take. Other areas I really try to avoid are sunken logs in swampy bits, around the edges of beaver lodges or where rocks are half-submerged — anywhere that the ice can warm up and weaken around the edges of objects. Even worse are areas where currents could exist: points jutting out or between islands, or where a lake narrows. If there's any chance of a current, then avoid it at all costs.

Large frozen lakes have an added danger — pressure cracks. Ice expands as it forms. You'll hear it groan as it thickens. As pressure builds and the ice is stressed, cracks will randomly form. Even high winds will shift the ice, pulling it apart or pushing it together. Open leads can form even if the ice is a meter thick. Many snowmobilers die, especially while traveling in the dark, due to pressure cracks. Traveling at fast speeds, they either fall through an open

It's safest to keep near the river's edge and avoid open water.

As evening temperatures drop, the ice expands, shrinks and cracks, sending out an eerie echoing boom across the lake. Photo: Claire Quewezence

lead or crash into an ice ridge. According to the Canadian Red Cross, 46 percent of snowmobilers' deaths resulted from immersion in open sections of ice.

Cold nights bring on an echoing boom as the ice expands, shrinks and cracks. It's normal — even though it gives you an incredible eerie feeling. Just be careful of water squeezing through the cracks.

River ice also has its own issues. A river does provide an excellent trail to lead you through the frozen woods. However, there's a lot of variables, like narrows and fast currents where the river will never freeze thick enough to be safe. It can be a deadly circumstance if you go through. The current can quickly take you under.

One of my past college students died this way. He was walking home after a late-night study group and chose the short section of the river to cross rather than a bridge further downstream. The current took him under when he fell through. They found his body two days later.

If you choose to travel on river ice, then make sure to keep to the edges where there's less flow and only on large rivers with little flow.

Yes, there are ways to get out if you fall through. However, you don't want to fall through!

Slush becomes extremely problematic when a camper is traveling over ice.

Slush

Slush, or overflow, is a convoluted issue. It happens when it snows and the weight places pressure on the ice. While the temperature changes, the ice shifts and cracks and with extra pressure from above, water is pushed up between the snow and ice. This creates very problematic slush pockets. The deeper the snow, the nastier the conditions. Your snowshoes or skis will bog down and your sled will stick like glue. It's like being caught in a big bowl of jello. You also risk getting a soaker, something you definitely don't want while winter trekking. The moment you get bogged down, try to head for solid ice or snow as quick as

possible. Use some form of scraper to remove the frozen sludge off your sled. When traveling in a group, spread out. The slush pocket will become worse with more people traveling through it. Snowshoes will help keep your weight evenly spread out, but the buildup of slush will make it feel like two cement blocks tied to your feet. On the bright side, a slush pocket is a great place to gather fresh water. Colder temperatures will eventually re-freeze the slush into ice and wind will help blow off the insulating snow. I find smaller lakes, protected from wind, are the worst for slush throughout the winter months.

Safety pointers for traveling on ice

- Always walk in single file and well-spread out when walking in groups.
- Stay clear of creek or river mouths where currents keep the ice from forming properly.
- Carry a long pole. You can use it to poke and check the ice as you go, as well as hold it horizontally in case you break through.
- Always have ice picks easily accessible while traveling across ice. You can buy them or simply make them out of a piece of hockey stick with nails driven into it. Ice picks are used, one in each hand, to help pull you out if you ever go through the ice.
- Pack a survival kit and keep it with you. It should contain an extra pair of clothes, waterproof matches or fire striker. Butane lighters don't work in the cold.
- If you do go through the ice, quickly start breaking the thin ice around you, spread your arms and legs to distribute your weight, pull yourself out and roll or wriggle like a seal onto neighboring ice. Kick your legs to help propel you on to the ice. Don't immediately stand up. You'll probably fall through again. Keep wriggling until you get to safer ice.
- Get out of the wind and get a fire going. Wrap yourself up in your sleeping bag or bivvy bag if you have your full gear with you.
- If you're assisting someone else that has gone through the ice, first consider whether it's safer to call for professional help or to do the rescue yourself.
- If possible, use a long pole or throw bag (rope). Lie down on the ice to distribute your weight while approaching the person.

Use a ski pole to continually test the ice conditions ahead of you.

The charm of fishing is that it is the pursuit of what is elusive but attainable, a perpetual series of occasions for hope.

—John Buchan

CHAPTER 12

Ice Fishing

I FIND IT ODD THAT MOST winter campers don't fish while on a trip. I grew up fishing with my father, and he'd role in his grave if I didn't wet a line while camping. Fishing adds to any trip. There's nothing like cooking up fresh fish after a few days of stomaching those pre-packaged, dehydrated meals. Of course, always have a back-up meal packed in case you don't get a bite. But if you're lucky enough to catch something, take note that the sooner you eat it, the better. Fish taste best when they are prepared within hours — or minutes — of catching them.

Fishing spots

The best spots to fish in the winter are generally the same as in the summer: off rocky points, between islands and along weedy shorelines. Naturally, finding those spots can be difficult in the winter. It's a bonus if you know the lake and have fished it before when it wasn't frozen over. If not, make sure to keep moving and try various places. That's the key to success. It's also important to note that fish are slower in the winter. They're harder to locate, but when you do find them, they're usually all gathered together and ready to be caught.

Early in the winter and later in the season are the best times to catch more fish. It's all about oxygen. In the early part of the winter season (late November to the middle of December), the aquatic plants consume carbon dioxide and give out oxygen. Fish, especially

Make sure to pack an ice auger. The more holes you make, the better chance of catching a fish.

species like trout, are drawn to this process. As the days shorten, sunlight lessens, invertebrates break down the underwater vegetation and consume oxygen, and snow loads on the ice block out the sun. As such, there's far less oxygen created, and the fish go into a sort of slumber. This process goes into reverse as the winter begins to break, and the fishing gets better. So, if you're fishing mid-winter you need to tease and taunt the fish as much as possible.

Techniques

There are two main techniques while ice fishing: jigging with a small rod and reel combo, or fishing stationary with a tip up. I usually head out to jig in early morning and in the evening, and I set up a tip-up to watch during the day.

Tip-ups are a lazy way of ice fishing. They allow you to fish without sitting at one hole and jigging constantly. It's also a great way to fish various holes and try different depths at once. Tip-ups are rigged with a bright flag that pops up when a fish takes your bait. That means, of course, you need to use scented plastic or live or frozen bait.

I prefer tip-ups made of metal or wood; plastic ones break too easily.

An ice scoop comes in handy to keep the ice hole open.

I prefer tip-ups made of metal or wood. I find plastic ones break too easily in cold temperatures. I also like the designs where the spool of line is underwater, keeping it from freezing. Orange flags are easier to see than yellow, and I've painted my wooden tip-ups a bright color to help keep an eye on them while I sit at camp enjoying a hot tea.

Both jigging and tip-ups are effective, but as a rule, jigging will catch you more fish. You want to jig just off the bottom, about an inch. Lower your line until it reaches bottom, raise it up slightly, and then jig it up and down. If you are jigging, make sure you don't overdo it.

Don't jig too vigorously. Twitch the bait with your wrist or slowly move it up and down by raising and lowering your forearm. Make sure to always feel the weight of the jig so you can detect a strike when it happens. When the fish does bite, set the hook with a steady, not jerky, upward lift. If you're fishing for pan fish, lessen your pound-test on your line and your jig size. Four pound-test is standard for fish like perch or crappie. Eight pound-test is for lake trout and walleye.

Some of my favorite jigs for trout and walleye are vertical Williams Nipigon, EGB and Swedish Pimple, as well as horizontal minnow baits like Jigging Raps, Jigging Shad Raps and Rapala Snap Raps.

My favorite fish recipes

Sure, you could just clean what you've caught and cook it, but where is the fun in that? Even when camping in the winter months, you shouldn't sacrifice flavor. Below, I've included some of my crowd-pleasing dishes to prepare with freshly-caught fish.

Herb-stuffed Grilled Crappie in Lime Sauce

juice and zest from 1 lime
2 tbsp. olive oil or canola oil
1 glove garlic, diced
2 fresh Crappie or Perch fillets
4 fresh dill branches
4 stalks chives
canola oil
salt and pepper

At camp: Thaw lime sauce, if frozen. Clean and fillet fish. Pat dry with paper towels. Place dill and chives along the length of one fish fillet. Top with second fillet; rub fish lightly with oil. Wrap in foil, secure tightly. Cook over medium-hot coals or on a lightly oiled grill rack for 10 minutes, or until fish is opaque and flakes easily with a fork. Season to taste with salt and pepper. Serve the fish drizzled with lime sauce.

Caribbean Brook Trout

Fillets of 1 brook trout (a small lake
    trout or rainbow trout will do the
    job as well)
wooden skewers
2 lemons
1 small bag (100 g) jalapeno plantain
    chips
1 tbsp olive oil
Pinch kosher salt
Pinch black pepper
Mango salsa (dehydrated):
    1 cup frozen mango chunks
    1 tbsp olive oil
    2 tbsp red pepper, diced small
    Few drops Tabasco sauce
    Pinch kosher salt
    Pinch dried thyme

At camp: Mix chips, oil and pepper
in a bowl or Ziploc bag and crush into
small pieces. Cut trout into chunks
and place 3 to 4 chunks on each
skewer. Dip fish in chip mix and wrap
in tinfoil. Cook over heat for 5 minutes
per side and cover with lemon and
mango salsa.

Spanish Perch

2-3 perch fillets
2 sausages
¼ cup olive oil
1 onion, sliced
2 cloves garlic, finely chopped
1 red pepper (dehydrated)
½ cup diced leeks (dehydrated)
1 cup long-grain rice
2 cups water
1 can (443 ml) chopped tomatoes
    (dehydrated)
Pinch saffron
Pinch salt
½ cup peas (frozen or dehydrated)

At camp: Cut perch into chunks and
add to an oiled pan on medium heat.
Add onion and sausage. When meat
browns, add garlic, red pepper, leeks
and peas and sauté for one minute.
Add to cooked rice and simmer for 20
minutes.

Baked Pecans and Walleye

4 walleye fillets
1 tbsp olive oil
½ cup whole pecans
Pinch salt and pepper
12 Breton Original crackers (or anything
    that resembles them)
Cucumber salsa (made at home and
    dehydrated):
    ½ English cucumber, finely diced
    1 large tomato
    2 tbsp olive oil
    1 tbsp chopped cilantro
    1 tsp finely chopped garlic
    3 drops Tabasco sauce
    A dash of salt and black pepper

At home: Mix ingredients for cucumber salad, dehydrate and store in a Ziploc bag.

At camp: Mix olive oil, pecans, salt, pepper and crackers. Crumble mixture until it resembles coarse breadcrumbs. Roll walleye in crumbled mixture and place on in Tinfoil. Bake over coals for 8-10 minutes and top with dehydrated cucumber salsa.

Santa Fe Fish Cakes

1 lb walleye or pike
1 cup all-purpose flour
2 cups dried potatoes flakes
2 tbsp cilantro
1 tsp dehydrated jalapeno pepper
½ tsp dried onion
½ cup cornmeal
1 egg white or ½ cup powdered egg
1 cup dehydrated salsa
½ tsp salt
½ tsp pepper

At camp: In a small pot, combine reconstituted potatoes flakes, fish pieces, cilantro, jalapeno, onion, salt and pepper. Divide contents into small bundles and shape them into round cakes. Dredge in flour. Dip them in egg whites (or reconstituted powdered egg). Dredge them again in cornmeal. Bake in deep-dish frying pan or Outback Oven for 20 minutes. Reconstitute salsa sauce in 1/4 cup boiling water and serve on top of fish cakes.

Baked Trout Amandine

4 small brook trout
¼ cup bread crumbs
¼ cup finely chopped almonds
1 lemon
½ tsp pepper
1 tbsp dried lemon thyme
1 tbsp dried sage

At camp: In a small pot, combine bread crumbs, almonds, lemon thyme, sage and pepper. Mix well. Sprinkle contents of pot over skin side of gutted trout. Roll trout in tin-foil with slices of lemon and bake directly in the in coals of a campfire for 15 minutes.

I was never lost in the woods in my whole life,
though once I was confused for three days.
—Daniel Boone

CHAPTER 13

Map and Compass

"WHY NOT JUST PACK A GPS?" That's usually the first question I get when I give a workshop on map and compass navigation. It's a fair question. Most people have become used to finding their way with a Global Positioning System (GPS), and it's something I end my workshops (and this chapter) with. Knowing how to use a map and compass first, however, makes the GPS part of the workshop a breeze. Understanding how a GPS works is second nature once the students are familiar with map and compass navigation.

Maps

Reading a map — matching what's on the paper to what's in front of you — is a lost art. I blame the GPS. Too many people are glued to their device rather than looking at what's around them. I also blame less time playing in the woods, especially as children. People just don't get out exploring enough to learn how to read a landscape. Map reading, however, is a crucial part for traveling outdoors. Even though I pack a compass and GPS, I rarely make use of them. But I'm constantly checking my map to help get from point A to point B.

Not only are maps critical to navigating while you're out there, they also act as an excellent resource while planning your trip back home. I've spent countless hours glancing over maps. I'll trace out a possible route and then unfold the same map a week later and inevitably discover another trip idea.

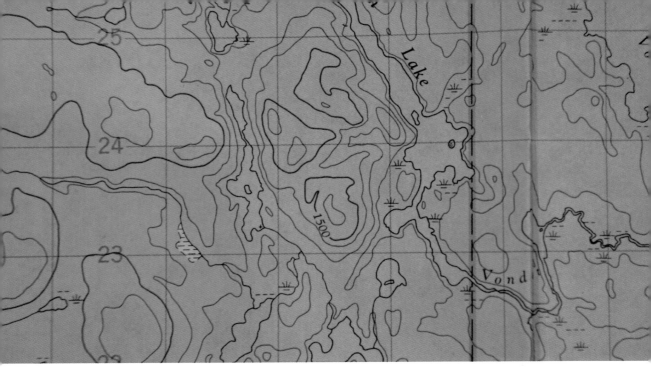

The closer the wavy brown contour lines are on the map, the steeper the terrain.

Maps aren't simply landscapes, they're dreamscapes, each one having all kinds of adventures hidden amongst its contour lines. Looking at them is simply addictive.

Choosing which map to pack depends entirely on where you're headed. If tripping in well-known parks, a detailed map produced by the park itself is usually good enough. Park-produced maps are more up-to-date and designed specifically for your purpose. However, in non-regulated parks or other less traveled areas, you need to bring topographic maps.

The detail of each topographical map is judged by its scale. The smaller the scale is, the less detail that is shown. They range from 1:10,000 to 1:100,000. For back-country use, the most common scale is 1:50,000, meaning 1 cm (3/8 in.) on the map is equivalent to 500 m (1600 ft.) on the ground. This scale size covers the most ground per map and still has enough suitable information, saving you a lot of money in the long run. However, if you require more detail on a specific area (i.e. a hill top or cliff face) then use the 1:250,000 scale.

Apart from marking the location of lakes, rivers, rapids, falls, roads, trails, etc., the most useful part of a topographic map is the wavy brown lines on the map, called "contour lines," that denote the topography of the land. Each line marks where the position of the land is above sea level. Every fifth

ESTIMATING DISTANCE ON A MAP

Judging distance on a map can be done by simply counting the number of quadrants (squares formed by vertical and horizontal UTM lines). Each one is equivalent to 1000 m in length.

contour line, called an "index contour," has the elevation marked somewhere along its length. Each type of map may vary, but the vertical height between each interval is usually 10 m (approximately 50 ft). So, the closer the lines are together, the steeper the grade.

Compasses

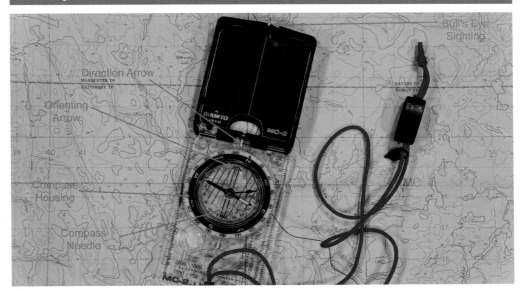

An orienteering compass comes with a preset declination screw.

I made good use of my compass while working as a Forest Technician in northern Ontario. The model was a regular orienteering compass, complete with a magnetic-tipped needle, a compass housing marked with an orienteering arrow and orienteering lines, a graduated dial, a base plate which doubles as a ruler (measuring in inches and centimeters), and an index line. However, it also had a few extra gizmos, like a preset declination (a must in my opinion) and a mirror with a "bull's eye" on top so you can read a bearing while holding the compass at eye level (and check your hair in the morning).

Declination

The first thing to note when using a compass is that the red end of the floating arrow always points to "magnetic" north, not "true" north. Since the needle is magnetized, it points toward the earth's magnetic field (made up of molten iron). To help confuse the issue, however, this is a different place than "true" north or what's better known as the "geographical" North Pole. The difference in degrees between these two northern points is called "declination." To confuse the issue even further, the amount of compass error (declination) is not only dependent on where you are on the earth, it also changes on a yearly basis. This variance is usually only a few degrees (30 degrees is the largest), but the further you follow it, the more you're going to head off in the wrong direction.

To compensate for declination, you must first check what the declination is for the area you are traveling in. One way to do this is to contact the government agency for that area (Ministry of Natural Resources, Department of Mines, Department of the Interior, etc.) and just ask. Or just Google it. It's also noted on the margins of a topographic map (usually the upper right-hand corner). Look for a sketch of three arrows: True North (TN), Grid North (GN), Magnetic North (MN). TN marks 360 degrees (0 degrees). GN represents parallel vertical lines as seen on the topo map. MN is marked to either the left (west) or right (east) of the TN arrow, with the variation of degrees shown between TN and GN. You actually want the variation between TN and MN, so either use what's given, since the amount

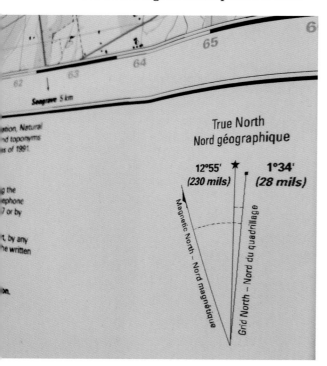

The difference in degrees between true north and magnetic north is called "declination."

between TN and GN is never that much to worry about, or add or subtract the difference.

It's best to own a compass with a declination screw. You can reset the declination by turning the screw (west or east) to the proper degree and never have to worry about it the entire trip. If you don't have a declination screw, then you're going to have to do some math to help you find your way. Remember the phrase: "east is least, and west is best." If the declination is to the east, then you would subtract the amount of degrees to your bearing. If the declination is to the west, then you would add it to your bearing. So, if the declination was 10 degrees W, and your bearing was 42 degrees, then you would follow 52 degrees. If the declination was 10 degrees E, and your bearing was 42 degrees, then you would follow 32 degrees. This is where having a declination screw comes in handy. Sounds confusing, which is why the declination already adjusted on your compass is a good idea; you'll never have to add or subtract each time you take a separate bearing.

Taking a field bearing

A field bearing is a degree (heading) calculated without the aid of a topographic map. This technique isn't used that often anymore. Mostly you keep an eye on the map and use obvious land forms (i.e. islands, large hills, creek mouths) to keep on track. But let's say you find yourself confused while crossing a big frozen lake, and you want to stay in the right direction. Or how about when you just want to take a day hike up a ridge you've spotted from your campsite? Here's how you do it:

1. Hold your compass level, at chest height.
2. Point the direction-of-travel arrow (the top of the compass) at the point you want to go (i.e. other side of the lake or a particular ridge top).
3. Rotate the compass housing (the round dial with all the degrees marked on it) until the orienteering arrow (the one that doesn't float) is perfectly lined up with the compass needle (the red pointed arrow that floats).
4. Read off the bearing (set in degrees) that is lined up with the direction-of-travel arrow.
5. Keep following that bearing by constantly aiming off on an object ahead; put the compass away, walk to the object, take the compass back out, and aim off another object.
6. To get back to where you once were, just figure out the reciprocal (the opposite bearing). This can be found by either subtracting 180 degrees from your previous heading or looking at where the other end of the red needle is pointing.

Map and Compass Skills

Using a map and compass together is the technique used to figure out how to get from point A to point B. The compass, used similarly to a protractor, gives you a reassuring line to follow on your map, and it is the main reason why anyone traveling outdoors would unpack their compass in the first place. Just follow these basic steps:

1. Place the map on a relatively flat service.
2. Mark the letter A on the map to indicate where you are and then mark B where you want to go on the map.
3. Line up the side of the compass' base plate from A to B (route of travel), making sure the direction-of-travel arrow (top of the compass) is pointing to B.
4. Without moving the compass, rotate the compass housing (the round dial with all the degrees marked on it) until the orienteering arrow points north and the orienteering lines (inside the housing) run parallel with the north and south lines (UTM) on the map.
5. Read out the bearing marked at the direction-of-travel arrow. (Take note that since you are using the compass like a protractor, you can ignore the compass needle during the entire procedure.)
6. Lift the compass off the map and make the correction for declination to the bearing. (if you don't have the compass already adjusted by a declination screw.)
7. Hold the compass at chest height and rotate your body until the floating magnetic needle lines up with the orienteering arrow. The compass is now pointing to B.
8. To calculate the distance between A and B, make use of the bar scale given at the bottom of the map. You can also get a quicker estimate by just counting the number of (UTM) quadrants (square boxes) on the route. Each quadrant measures 1 km.

Triangulation

Each bit of information I have offered so far tells you how to avoid getting lost. But what if you already are? Or, what if you're even just a little confused as to your whereabouts? For example, what if you're on a small island on a large frozen lake that contains many small islands, but you have no idea which one?

The method to find where you are is called "triangulation." Here's how it's done:

1. Look around and try to recognize at least two prominent landmarks (i.e. a high rocky ledge, a large bay or inlet or a fire tower).
2. Search out those landmarks on your topographic map.
3. Take a field bearing for both landmarks.
4. Correct for declination.
5. Calculate the reciprocal by either subtracting 180 degrees or just looking at the degree marked on the opposite end of the orienteering arrow.
6. Using your compass as a protractor, consider the two landmarks on your topographic map as A and B, draw a line out from each, and where they meet is where you are standing.

Offsets for obstacles

Offsetting is a technique used to detour around an obstacle while maintaining your course. After all, how possible would it be to follow a heading without running into some type of barrier, like open water or slush on a frozen lake? A deliberate offset is done by moving at right angles for a given distance. For example, if you are following a heading of 360 degrees (due north), and you come across an obstacle, you would then follow a right angle (90 degrees) for 20 paces (or whatever distance would allow you to get around the obstacle). Then, you would again follow your previous heading (360 degrees), until you get to the other side of the pond. To get yourself back on track you then take the opposite right angle (270 degrees) for 20 paces.

TOP 5 MAP AND COMPASS ERRORS

1. Magnetic needle is affected by nearby magnetic materials (i.e. belt buckle, hydro lines, wire fence, lead pencil, etc.)
2. A large air bubble can form in the compass housing, causing a considerable amount of readout error.
3. Taking a reading off the wrong end of the magnetic needle. Remember, the red arrow is north!
4. When placing the compass on the map to get a heading, the compass housing is turned so that north is pointing to the bottom end (south) of the map rather than top (north). It should be the other way around.
5. Having your compass placed on a map pointing from A (start) to B (finish) and not B (finish) to A (start).

GPS (Global Positioning System)

Global Positioning Systems (GPS) makes correcting for declination on your compass a thing of the past.

Global Positioning Systems (GPS) have come a long way. I remember back in the early 1990s, the models we used in the field while working in forestry were massive, and the possible error could be off 200 m. We still thought the contraption was awesome! Now look at us. Most cars have GPS navigation, and it's rare to find a camper who doesn't have a high tech navigational device packed away. The cost has dropped in half. The receiver itself is more accurate and can now determine your position within 10 m. Problems with correcting for declination on your compass is a thing of the past. You can also enter map coordinates (latitude and longitude), and the receiver will provide a compass bearing, the distance and the time required to get to the desired location. And its best ability is to punch in your present position, save it as a waypoint and allow you to easily find your way back home, record a favorite campsite

> **SKILLS ARE MORE IMPORTANT THAN TECHNOLOGY**
> An over reliance on technology dulls your sense of spatial awareness and robs you of the ability to accurately place yourself on a map. With a map and compass, your eyes must constantly dart from map, to bearing, to feature and back, leading to greater spatial awareness and directional knowledge. With a GPS, one simply looks at their tracking position and requires less reliance on surrounding features for placement.
> —Brad Jennings, Forestry Specialist and Extreme Weather Camper

or even mark a productive fishing hole.

GPS are based on three separate parts: a network of satellites orbiting the earth that sends out electromagnetic frequencies (radio waves), a number of control stations that track and control the satellites, and the GPS unit itself, which receives the satellite signal and calculates your position by using latitude and longitude or UTM coordinates.

Where a GPS becomes an excellent tool is when you want to quickly find a bearing to a given point or the act of triangulation is next to impossible with just a map and compass due to the lack of obvious landmarks.

With that said, a GPS does not replace a good map and compass. Remember, if you do not know how to navigate with a map and compass, not only does it become impossible to use a GPS properly, you also won't have a clue how to follow the instruction manual when you buy one. Basically, if you don't know

how to navigate without a GPS, you'll be just as hopeless with one. You can't run before you walk.

Understanding the Universal Transverse Mercator (UTM)

The Universal Transverse Mercator (UTM) is a grid system developed by the military in the 1960s during the Cold War to find submarines. It's a much easier system for locating areas on a map than the traditional longitude and latitude system, especially when using a GPS. The Global Positioning System can give coordinates in both Latitude/Longitude and UTM.

Using your phone as a GPS

Your cell phone can act as a GPS device. It works by finding satellites, and you don't need a Wi-Fi signal — the GPS works off the satellites, not a cell tower. But you'll need to download a map app on your phone - Gaia APP seems to be one of the best.

CHAPTER 14

Tree and Animal Identification

Winter twig and bark identification

IT MAKES A BIG DIFFERENCE to your camping experience if you know at least some tree species: ones that get a fire going quickly and ones that burn the most British thermal units (BTUs). The more BTUs a species of wood produces when it burns, the more heat it gives off. A lot of people panic about twig identification. My college students, who I teach part-time, sure do. It's not all that difficult, however. In fact, I find it easier to identify a tree from its winter twig than its summer leaf. It's basically like putting together a puzzle, making up simple ways to help remember specific details about each species.

To start with, you can break down deciduous (hardwood) twigs into two categories: opposite branching and alternate branching. Some species, like ash and maple, have their lateral buds (the bud on the side of the twig) opposite to each other. Most species, however, are alternate, meaning lateral buds are interspersed on the twig. The shape, size, texture and color are all different for each species. Most buds also have protective scales that protect their leaf tissue, and each species has a different shape, pattern and number of scales.

White Ash

Black Ash

White Ash
Million BTUs per cord = 23.6
Black Ash
Million BTUs per cord = 18.7

There's no other terminal bud (top bud on the twig) that looks like an ash. To me it resembles a horse's hoof. The lateral buds, which are close to touching the terminal bud, have a little happy 'smile.' They are also opposite branching, meaning one bud is opposite to the other. For white ash, the color of the bud is light brown and the twig has a dull gun-blue shine to it.

Black ash has the same horse's hoof on the terminal bud and smile on the lateral, but the terminal bud is chocolate brown (it looks like a Hershey Kiss chocolate) and the twig is a light brown to gray color. The lateral buds are also further down from the terminal bud. Black ashes love their feet wet and will grow in wet areas. White ashes are upland and dry.

Sugar Maple
Million BTUs per cord = 24
Red Maple
Million BTUs per cord = 18.1

The twigs on the sugar maple are set in another opposite branching arrangement. All maples' twigs are. The terminal bud is slender, pointed, and has several scales along it. It also has two lateral buds sticking out of each side. It's like the devil wearing a dunce hat. The twig is reddish up on top but turns

Red Maple

Red Oak

White Oak

buds. The red oak has red pointy buds and the white oak has roundish light-brown buds.

White Birch
Million BTUs per cord = 20.2

Yellow Birch
Million BTUs per cord = 21.8

White birch is easily recognized by its white birch bark, but it doesn't gain that outer bark until it gets bigger. To identify it when the birch is a sapling, look for buds that have a gummy green and chestnut brown color. The

White Birch

Yellow Birch

brownish-blond soon after.

The red maple is similar to the sugar maple, but with blunt terminal and lateral buds and less scales. The twig is totally red in color. This tree has softer wood than a sugar maple and a worse burn rate. It's readily available in low swampy areas, however, and usually contains a lot of dead wood.

Red Oak
Million BTUs per cord = 24

White Oak
Million BTUs per cord = 24

The alternate branching arrangement of buds and the terminal "cluster" of buds are great identification features. Both the red oak and the white oak have a number of terminal buds grouped together. That's why deer love browsing on them. One bite of the twig's top and the deer gets multiple twig is dull red-brown with numerous white lenticels along it (it looks like it has been sprinkled with salt, like a pretzel).

Mature yellow birches have flaky yellow bark, not white. The buds are similar to white birch but lack the greenish part, and the twigs lack the lenticels. If you really want to know the difference, yellow birch tastes like wintergreen gum, white birch just tastes like a piece of wood.

Basswood
Million BTUs per cord = 13.5
One of the softest hardwoods, the bark feels like cork when you push your thumbnail into it. . The bud is big, round and red like a Christmas light bulb. It's not the best for burning due to its soft wood fibers.

Ironwood

Ironwood
Million BTUs per cord = 26.8
It's a slender tree that doesn't grow too large. The buds are a green-brown color, short and a little hairy. The twigs are dark reddish-brown with no hair, but start off being pale green with hair. Its bark is the easiest feature to identify. It's flaky and comes off in loose strips, like bacon frying in a skillet. It's called ironwood because of the hardness of its wood — I've seen sparks fly out from my chainsaw while cutting it. Pioneers even used it for wagon axles.

Trembling Aspen
Million BTUs per cord = 18
This is the most common poplar to be found in the woods. It's a weed tree, growing fast and dying young. It's also a poor species for burning due to its loose, fibrous wood. The buds are long

Basswood

Trembling Aspen

Beech

and "hug" the twig. From a distance, a stand of them resembles birch trees — they have smooth yellowish bark.

(I got paid as a consultant on a film set once by simply checking out an opening scene of a group of white birch. The film was a documentary on the days of the voyageurs, and they showed the construction of birchbark canoes. Good thing I checked — they filmed trembling aspen instead. They were very thankful, and paid me a large bonus.)

Beech
Million BTUs per cord = 24
My students at risk (troubled youth who have decided to go back to school) say this bud looks like a marijuana joint. It kind of does — or at least a skinny cigar. The buds are widely divergent from the stem, looking like

thorns. The bark of the tree is a key feature: smooth and gray like an elephant's trunk. Beech trees have a tendency to hold on to their leaves in the winter. The stem bases don't fully form the common corky layer, which would push off the fall leaves. The first settlers were known to use these bronze-colored, dried winter beech leaves to stuff their sleeping mats to help keep warm.

Balsam Fir
Million BTUs per cord = 14.3
The needles have a flattened appearance and two dull white lines on the underbelly. They are fully attached around the twig but appear flat. It's a popular Christmas tree because of its pleasant odor and hardy needles staying on the branch.

Balsam fir can be used for so many things in the winter. The boughs make

Balsam Fir

Hemlock

differences, however, are that they actually grow flat on the twig and that the two white lines on the underbelly are far more prominent. The bark also doesn't have resin blisters. It's smoothly furrowed, with a purplish tint on mature trees, and scaly on younger trees.

Tamarack

Million BTUs per cord = 20.8

The eastern larch (tamarack) is the one species that totally messes up the term 'evergreen.' It's a deciduous conifer, meaning it loses its needles in the fall. So if you see what looks like a dead conifer during the winter, it's probably a tamarack in its dormant stage. The needles, when present, are short and grow in tufts. Look at the buds to determine if it is alive. The bark has a dark reddish-orangish hue to it and is very scaly, similar to spruce.

excellent bedding, the lower dead branches make excellent kindling, and the resin blisters along the bark (looking like pimples on a pre-teen) can be squeezed and the pitch used for a fire starter or placed on a cut to act like a bandage. If you hear the balsam fir crack in the cold, then you know it's darn cold. All but one of the coniferous tree species, the tamarack, don't lose their leaves in the fall due to having a thick resin that can't freeze as easily as sap in a deciduous tree (maple, ash, beech). However, when temperatures go below –40°, the thick resin will begin to solidify and you'll hear conifer trees crack as the wood fibers expand.

Hemlock

Million BTUs per cord = 15.9

The needles look similar to balsam fir needles on the twig. The two big

Tamarak

Eastern White Cedar

The wood makes amazing fuel for fires. It has a similar BTU value to white birch — basically, it's a hard softwood, just as poplar is considered a soft hardwood. I'd choose it over pine or spruce if you're camped in a forest mostly made up of conifers. Natives have used it for building toboggans and snowshoes because of its dense wood fibers.

Eastern White Cedar
Million BTUs per cord = 12.2
The needles look like fish scales, with an opposite branching arrangement on the twig, and grow in flattened sprays. Nothing else looks like it. The wood is highly resinous, which makes it exceptional kindling. Many Native groups translate the name of the tree as the "tree of life" for its medicinal use and help in getting a fire going.

Black Spruce
Million BTUs per cord = 15.9
White Spruce
Million BTUs per cord = 21.6
The main difference between the black and white spruce is their overall shape.

Black spruce trees grow tall and narrow, as opposed to conical like white spruce. There's usually a knobby clump of growth on top. The needles are blunter than those of the white spruce, and black spruce is usually found rooted in wet areas; it dominates the northern boreal forest. The white spruce is conical in shape with no knob on top and lighter-colored needles.

Black Spruce

White Spruce

Jack Pine

Red Pine

Jack Pine

Million BTUs per cord = 17.1

Its needles come in bundles of two, and are short and twisted. But it's the cones of the jack pine that really help identify it. They're curved inwards, usually in pairs, and most stay closed until opened by the heat of a forest fire. If you throw them in the campfire, they'll pop like popcorn. To me, they look like poop on a stick.

Scots Pine

Million BTUs per cord = 17.1

The needles look similar to those of the jack pine, but there are no curved, closed cones. The upper bark has a prominent orange color.

Red Pine

Million BTUs per cord = 17.1

These needles grow in clusters of two, like a peace sign, and are longer and stiffer at 6 inches (15 cm). A bundle of needles makes an excellent pot scrubber. The bark has large scales or plates, and is reddish all the way along its length.

White Pine

Scots Pine

White Pine

Million BTUs per cord = 17.1

The only pine tree that has its needles in bundles of five, not two; they're soft to the touch. The outline or silhouette is a main identifying feature. They aren't conical, but rather grow out and upwards. My students at risk say it looks like the white pine is "flipping you the bird." Heck, whatever helps them identify it.

Animal Tracking

While you're out in the woods in winter, you have the opportunity to follow and understand animal tracks in the snow — nothing like this is possible in summer.

Picking up animal poop and following their tracks in the snow was one of the best jobs I've ever had. I worked as a wildlife technician for a regional conservation authority and spent many days wandering around the winter woods, studying species and putting their story together. That's what you do while tracking an animal: try to tell their story. You follow their prints, study their scat and figure out what they've been up to, what they've been eating. And, if you're lucky, really lucky, you'll even get a glimpse of the animal you're tracking.

One particular job was to look into coyotes overharvesting white-tailed deer. The premise was that coyote populations were too high and they were eating way too many deer. I headed out to gather the story, to prove or disprove the hypothesis.

Two months of field work had me tracking a total of seven coyotes

It's rare to actually spot the coyote you've been tracking all day.

Fox tracks are similar to cat tracks. Sniff around for the pungent smell of their urine. It smells like watered-down skunk spray.

— all of which I named and all from which I gathered enough poop to debunk the theory that they were eating too many deer. I never once caught a glimpse of them, but I got to know their every movements. They were eating more voles, mice and rabbit than deer. The majority of deer deaths were due to vehicles hitting them along a major highway. It was an interesting case study, all done by tracking and never once actually seeing a single coyote.

Tracking is a skill that takes many years to perfect. There's just too many variables, too many possibilities. Sometimes figuring out whether a print is a wolf, coyote or big dog just ends up being guesswork. There is a process to better your guesswork, however. With that said, I've never met a good but arrogant tracker. All serious trackers are humble and never claim an absolute identification.

Start by listing the animal's gait. It's the manner in which the animal is moving. The four main walking gaits are diagonal, pacer, bounder and galloper. An animal's gait can change; for example, a diagonal walker such as a deer can become a bounder when running. But the four main walking gaits can at least get you started.

Porcupines are pacers and leave a drag mark in the snow, which often includes the odd needle that has fallen from their bristly tail.

Diagonal pattern includes the deer, cat and dog families. It's the movement a human would make if it was moving on all fours; front right-arm and rear-left leg followed by front left-arm and rear right-leg, just like how a baby crawls across the floor.

Pacers are the opposite of diagonal walkers. They move their front and rear feet of one side at the same time. So, left front and left back together, then front right and back right together. Bears fit into this family. So do porcupines and raccoons. Skunks are also in this group, even though they are members of the weasel family and should walk like a bounder.

Bounders include animals in the weasel family and walk by stepping with both front feet followed by the rear feet. They basically "hop," placing both front feet down together then both back feet.

Gallopers are similar to bounders. Front feet land first, then the back feet. But the hind feet land in front of the front. Imagine squatting on the floor and placing your arms under you, with your feet first. That's how a galloper lands. They include rabbits, hares, and rodents. The key print mark of rabbits or hares are the front feet slightly off-kilter; a rodent's prints, like a squirrel, are parallel to each other.

Scat

An animal's feces tell wonders. They show what it's been eating as well as its overall health. In a canine species you'll see hair, bone, seeds. Moisture content also tells how long ago the animal passed through, something that's far more difficult with tracks. Just make sure not to get sick by breathing in dust particles from animal scat.

River otter scat is wet and clumpy and has to be some of the oddest and most intriguing out there, mainly because of the so-descriptive pile of non-digested material it leaves behind: reddish external skeletons of crayfish, jagged fish bones (that's gotta hurt), and lots of fish scales. You have to wonder if its diet is working for it at all. Fish scales are even so intact that biologists collect them, age them and determine the levels of PCBs the otter were digesting.

Species such as dogs, bears, raccoons, wolves, and coyotes have tubular shape scat. Wolves' scat measures approximately 4 inches (10 cm) and looks pretty much similar to dog poop at first glance, but upon close examination you'll see it's made up of bone chips and mats of fur, tapered at one end and held together with mucus.

Cats' feces are more tapered and foxes' are tapered at both ends (fox urine also smells like a dulled-down skunk spray). Cougars' scat is segmented, just under an inch long, with the ends rounded more than canines and maybe a few tufts of hair mixed in with it. The kicker, however, is that the poop is rarely found out in the open. Like all cats, cougars like to scratch a bit of dirt or snow on top of their poop and top it off with a sprinkle or two of urine. It's a territorial thing. To help you with the analysis, just remember back when you played in the sandbox as a kid and dug up a round, segmented piece of clay. It wasn't clay. It was cat poop. Cougar poop looks the same, but is bigger and definitely smellier.

Rabbits' scat looks like M&Ms, and rodents leave pieces of pencil lead. Moose leave woody capsule-shaped pellets and deer look more like large brown jelly beans. Porcupines leave enlarged, more roundish pellets.

Owls lack acid in their stomach to help digestion. That means they can't digest the bits of fur, feathers or bone in their food. They regurgitate "cough balls" that contain the non-digested bits. It's similar to scat. If you find owl pellets, you can pretty much guarantee that the bird will return to the same roost. They regurgitate in an area they feel safe.

Wolves and coyotes walk in a direct register, above left, while the domesticated dog wanders in an indirect pattern, above right.

Dog vs. wolf register

Once you know the difference between a rabbit and squirrel track, then it's time to move on to something more complicated: identifying the difference between a domesticated dog and a wolf. The key difference is in its register — the pattern of the tracks in the snow. If it's a direct register, the tracks will be in a straight line. As the animal lifts its front foot up, its rear foot drops directly into the front foot print. It's an adaptation to take advantage of the packed-down snow made by the front foot. This is also very common with coyotes, fox and cats. Domesticated dogs, however, are scattered. Dogs wander and sniff everything, totally distracted, acting like a cartoon character. Wolves move with purpose. Scat is also a major identification feature. Wolf poop will have bits and pieces of its prey (fur, bone, feathers) and dogs will have, well, bits and pieces of kibble.

Habitat

Looking at the surroundings will give you a bundle of clues. The dog vs. wolf, for example. Would wolves even be in the wooded area you're traveling? That's a key point to distinguish between a coyote and wolf. Match the habitat and region and make a logical guess of which one would it be.

Afterword

I'VE SCRAMBLED UP KILLARNEY PROVINCIAL PARK'S Silver Peak half-a-dozen times in the heat of the summer. It's a great view of stunted quartzite mounds and turquoise lakes. The hike also offers a crop of delicious blueberries growing at the peak and a dramatic view of a semi-wild landscape. The only problem, everyone seems to want a piece of it. On a summer hike it's common to share the walk with countless other hikers, all wanting to savor the solitude...and juicy blueberries.

So, when I was offered to join Lure of the North Outfitting (Kielyn and Dave Marrone) for a winter trek to the quartz-capped pinnacle in the frozen month of February, I jumped at the chance.

Our base camp was Clear Silver Lake, near the base of the summit, which we managed to reach by 4:00 p.m. the first day out. The walk in was uneventful, under blue skies with air temperatures that dropped to 10°F (–12°C) by late afternoon. It seemed too early to camp, but darkness comes soon in February and Dave and Kielyn immediately handed out jobs to everyone.

Whether setting up camp or tearing it down, it's imperative that everyone be given chores to do. All seasoned winter campers emphasize the importance of developing a disciplined routine. The second you become even a bit lethargic, the trip is doomed. Having something go unplanned on a summer trip usually isn't a big deal. Winter trips, however, a slight mistake can be deadly when temperatures reach below –4°F (–20°C) or so.

We split up chores. Some of us stomped down an area of snow for our communal eight-person hot tent. The others gathered wood. We brought down a dead standing cedar and hauled it in pieces back to camp to keep the wood stove going. Then we cut a hole in the lake ice for drinking water. Kielyn delivered some snacks and hot beverages before she started preparing dinner. We all settled into the cozy heated tent around 7:00 p.m.

The contrast between inside and outside temperatures was dramatic, like a meat locker and a Swedish sauna. It was a bitter −13°F (−25°C) outside and a toasty 77°F (25°C) inside. But with all of us making use of the same tent, we were soon taking turns savoring tea by the cook stove or heading outside to sip on single malt to relieve the claustrophobic feeling, gawk up at the glare of the full moon, and stand and listen to a nearby barred owl's famous "who cooks for you" call. A bunch of us even took a stroll out on the frozen lake, lay down on the ice and looked up at the stars while listening to the groan of the shifting ice underneath us.

The darker it got, got the colder it became, and the more conscious we were of our actions. Touching metal, for example: the moment your bare fingers made contact, you felt a searing sensation, and a slight frostnip. The surrounding forest turned brittle and black. It seemed almost menacing, especially when the trees cracked and popped due to left-over sap expanding in their trunks. As the temperature dropped to −18°F (−28°C), even light from our headlamps started to flicker, suffering from the effects of the cold.

It's not all disconcerting, however. Beyond the groaning ice and cracking tree sap, there was an absolute silence to the frozen landscape. We all loved it.

It was a tight squeeze having the seven of us sleep in one tent, but we enjoyed the camaraderie.

The plan was to have our first camp act as a base for two nights, giving us a full day to hike up Silver Peak. This stunted cap of quartzite is older than the Rockies, but not as high: a mere 1,781 feet (543 m), approximately the height of the CN Tower.

We should have hit the trail at first light. Problem was, while winter camping, it's impossible to just get up and go. There's wood to cut, the water hole to re-open and a good breakfast to consume — one with enough calories to keep our bodies warm throughout the day. We ended up strapping on our snowshoes and leaving camp around 9:30 a.m.

Travel was good at first. We definitely needed our snowshoes as the snow was well past our knees, but the temperature was moderate; we were down to wearing only our base layers an hour into the hike.

I was surprised how easy the trail

Evening calm on Clear Silver Lake.

was to follow. There was the odd blue trail marker nailed to a tree, but the trail itself was so well trodden that it wasn't difficult to stay on track. At the halfway point we had more tea, but the crew was starting to grow anxious about reaching the summit. The trail was getting steeper and our progress slower. Snow depth was getting to be an issue, going past our hips if we weren't wearing our snowshoes. By the time we had reached the three-quarter mark — a slab of rock where the trail makes a sudden twist to the southwest — it was 2:30 p.m. Doing the math, we realize it would be around 10:00 p.m. by the time we returned to base camp.

Feelings among the group were mixed. Rather than use the basic voting process, our outfitters stepped in and introduced a more favorable method called the five-finger rule. The process is quite simple; everyone closes their eyes and then holds up a count of fingers for the leaders to see. Holding up five fingers means you desperately want to reach the top of Silver Peak, no matter what; four represents that you're good to go to the top but could be convinced otherwise; three means you could easily be persuaded either way; two symbolizes a desire to head back; and one finger means you're eager to go back as soon as possible.

I was a tad unethical during the

Kielyn's turn at bat.

five-finger process and kept one eye open to take note of the outcome. What I saw was surprising. Everyone held up two fingers except myself. I chose five. The leaders then announced that a group decision was made to go back to base camp and not complete the hike to the top of Silver Peak.

I was pissed. I couldn't believe we were going back down after being so close to the summit. My reaction was out of character for me. I usually follow the rules and consider myself a group player. But not this time. I wanted to finish the climb, even if it meant I went alone and returned to camp in the pitch dark. My feelings may had something to do with an agreement I had made with a magazine prior to the trip to document a story of climbing up Silver Peak in the winter. Or maybe it was just blind arrogance. What ever the reason, I recommended the group

go back and I go on. This proposal went totally against the leader's voting procedure and my actions were entirely selfish. Besides that, it was obvious I had kept my eyes open during the referendum. I'm guessing that didn't sit well. But they all agreed and left me to continue on.

Gear was then re-arranged, packs were shouldered and snowshoes laced back up. Kielyn and Dave lead the others back down the hill and I continued trekking uphill. Literally two minutes into the walk up and guilt began creeping into my conscious. What was I thinking? I had gone against the golden rule of keeping good group dynamics while on a trip — I separated myself from the herd. I turned back — all of us leaving the summit of Silver Peak for another day. It was a full-fledged "group" expedition. Something far more important than reaching a frozen peak alone.

Returning with the entire crew was the best choice for the trip. Not only did it boost morale but by changing the trip's agenda we ended up having a better time the rest of the week. The remaining days were spent hiking up mini-versions of Silver Peak or playing a game of baseball out on the ice (snowshoes were used as bats and the ball was a gigantic roll of duct tape).

A true winter dreamscape enjoyed by all.

Further Reading

Aspen, Jean. *Arctic Daughter: A Wilderness Journey.* Crystal Lake, IL: Delta, 1993.

Batchelor, Bruce T. *Nine Dog Winter.* Victoria, BC: Agio, 2008.

Campbell, James. *The Final Frontiersman: Heimo Korth and His Family, Alone in Alaska's Arctic Wilderness.* New York: Atria, 2004.

Conover, Garrett & Alexandra Conover. *Snow Walker's Companion: Winter Camping Skills for the North.* Wrenshall, MN: Stone Ridge Press, 1994.

Henderson, Bruce. *Fatal North.* New York: Diversion, 2001.

Kochanski, Mors. *Bushcraft: Outdoor Skills and Wilderness Survival.* Edmonton, AB: Lone Pine Publishing, 1998.

Marchand, Peter. *Life in the Cold.* Lebanon, NH: University Press of New England, 1987.

Mears, Ray & Lars Fält. *Out on the Land: Bushcraft Skills from the Northern Forest.* London: Bloomsbury Publishing, 2016.

Merrick, Elliott. *True North: A Journey into Unexplored Wilderness.* Berkeley, CA: North Atlantic Books, 1989.

Olesen, Dave. *Kinds of Winter: Four Solo Journeys by Dogteam in Canada's Northwest Territories.* Waterloo, ON: Wilfred Laurier, 2014.

Osgood, William, and Leslie Hurley. *The Snowshoe Book.* New York: Penguin, 1983.

Owen, Joseph R. *Colder Than Hell: A Marine Rifle Company at Chosin Reservoir.* New York: Ballantine, 1997.

Proenneke, Richard. *One Man's Wilderness: An Alaskan Odyssey.* Anchorage: Alaska Northwest Books, 1973.

Rowlands, John J. *Cache Lake Country: Life In The North Woods.* New York: Countryman Press, 1998.

Rutstrum, Calvin. *Paradise Below Zero.* Minneapolis, MN: University of Minnesota, 1968.

Stuck, Hudson. *Ten Thousand Miles with a Dog Sled: A Narrative of Winter Travel in Interior Alaska.* New York: Cosimo Classics, 1914.

Wilkerson, James. *Hypothermia, Frostbite and Other Cold Injuries.* Seattle: Mountaineers, 1986.

Wilson, Hap. *The Cabin: A Search for Personal Sanctuary.* Toronto: Dundurn Press, 2005

Index